Enjoy! Sher

GENERATIONAL GURU

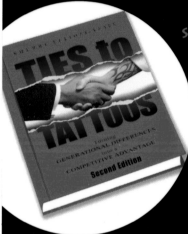

SHERRI ELLIOTT-YEARY

AUTHOR AND SPEAKER

ph: 214-802-2345

sherri@generationalguru.com

Visit my websites at:

GURU BLOG:
generationalguru.com

optimancestrategies.com

"Working out potential conflicts between the values and priorities of four generations in the workforce is not enough. Sherri Elliott recognizes the more complex issue of capitalizing on the talents of all to create a blended competitive advantage."

Sandra Yancey
Founder and CEO, eWomenNetwork, Inc.

"For the first time in history, four generations are sitting side by side in the workplace. Each generation has its own culture, defined by different events, standards, and values. Organizations must understand each generation to ensure they are optimizing their employees' contributions. This book shares the generational diversities and shows how to embrace them. There is a great sense of realism throughout the book, with a balanced viewpoint shown through examples of failures as well as successes. This is a must read, not just for HR professionals but also for anyone who manages people."

Jennifer Kaneshiro, PHR
Chief Human Resources Officer,
Chickasaw Nation Division of Commerce

"*Ties to Tattoos* provides thought-provoking realities you need to consider. It affords actionable ideas on how to gain better understanding of what drives today's workforce to deliver exceptional results."

George Killebrew
Senior Vice-President of Corporate Sponsorships,
Dallas Mavericks

"Capitalizing on the talents of a multigenerational workforce is the key to future business success. Sherri Elliott recognizes that and gives sound advice."

Leslie Elliott
President, Toni & Guy, USA

"Each generation has different values, different communication styles, and different opinions about what comes first: work or life. Generational diversity is a good thing, but it can also create perplexing challenges. *Ties to Tattoos* is a great resource to help you create a work environment filled with mutual respect and collaboration."

Nancy Barry
Speaker, Gen Y expert, and author of
When Reality Hits: What Employers Want
Recent College Graduates to Know

"I remember clearly the day I offered to pick up my niece at the airport. I told her to just call me when the plane landed. She hesitated and then asked, 'Can I just text you?' I realized she hesitated because she wasn't sure I knew how to text message and didn't want to be rude if I didn't. (I did.) I had to smile though, because this intergenerational exchange was just a microcosm of what's going on in workplaces every day. *Ties to Tattoos* provides helpful insights into the nature of and reasons for these generational differences and offers strategies for leveraging them to an organization's advantage.

While the commonalities between generations may be much greater than the differences, knowing how to recognize and manage the differences can make the leadership challenge less daunting."

Susan R. Meisinger, SPHR
Past President, Society for Human Resource Management

TIES to TATTOOS

TIES to TATTOOS

Turning
Generational Differences
into a
Competitive Advantage

Sherri Elliott

Brown Books Publishing Group
Dallas, Texas

Ties to Tattoos

Turning Generational Differences into a Competitive Advantage

© 2009 Sherri Elliott

Manufactured in the United States of America.

For information, please contact:

Brown Books Publishing Group

16200 North Dallas Parkway, Suite 170

Dallas, Texas 75248

www.brownbooks.com

972-381-0009

A New Era in Publishing™

Hardbound ISBN-13: 978-1-934812-30-3
Hardbound ISBN-10: 1-934812-30-7
Paperback ISBN-13: 978-1-934812-31-0
Paperback ISBN-10: 1-934812-31-5

LCCN: 2008942806

1 2 3 4 5 6 7 8 9 10

I would like to dedicate this book to my daughter Khirsten,
a Millenial. She is the light of my life and has taught me how to accept
her generation, even with body piercings!

Acknowledgments

First of all, I could not have done this without the love and support of my family and friends through this process of rediscovering myself.

Special thanks to my coach and mentor, Joanna Couch, who believed in me when I launched my business and stood beside me through this journey.

Thanks also to Lin O'Neill, who gave me the inspiration to write my first book and to Nilon who would not let me quit.

Although there is not enough room to name you all individually, I would like to thank the many friends and organizations who have willingly shared their special stories to help me shape this book.

Thank you to Sandra Yancey and Jennifer Kaneshiro. Your encouragement and friendship mean a lot to me.

Finally, a big thank-you to the great team at Brown Books Publishing Group—including Milli Brown, Kathryn Grant, Dr. Janet Harris, Latham Shinder, Cindy Birne, Cathy Williams, Rachel Felts, Bill Young, Jessica Kinkel, and Jennifer Allen, all of whom have contributed to helping my vision become a reality.

Contents

Foreword

Women instinctively connect with other women, especially if they share common interests, professions, and personal situations. Expanding networks to those with different interests, ages, and experiences can be a greater challenge. Now that kind of expansion is needed as four generations learn how not only to work together but also to form the competitive advantage essential in today's volatile business climate.

The same work/life balance that I have had to learn in my own professional and personal life now becomes vital in understanding the potential of four generations in the workforce. Traditionalists, Boomers, Xers, and Millennials see employment and their personal fulfillment in different ways. They respond to different motivations, work environments, and rewards. They also bring varied work ethics, talents, expertise with technology, and relationship skills. Savvy business leaders, managers, and human resource professionals recognize these differences and treat them as advantages.

Capitalizing on a multi-generational workforce within each organization is akin to expanding a network. Valuing skills, knowledge, and experience instead of concentrating on differences or seeming deficiencies can move a company toward success and equip it to survive and thrive in a dynamic business environment.

As women, we learn to listen to our own inner voices about what works for us. Corporations can turn inward, assess the competitive advantage already existing in the four generations of their workforce, and capitalize on all the profitable diversity they contain. *Ties to Tattoos* is a great place to begin.

Sandra Yancey
Founder and CEO, eWomenNetwork, Inc.

"Bob, meet Lars. He's the new
director of software development."

Chapter One

The Multigenerational Workplace Crisis

"As the employment market tightens, we're all out there competing
for the same person, the good ones, because we don't want them
going across the street to someone else while we're stuck with
mediocre people serving our clients."

—Jeff Powell, President
Razzoo's Cajun Café

*T*ies *to Tattoos* offers strategies for leveraging multigenerational differences in ways that make your company stronger. Understanding generational issues is one of the best new tools for resolving conflicts and boosting productivity. The people strategies described throughout this book, if applied in creative ways, will become the sustainable competitive business advantage for your company in the coming decade.

For the first time in history, the American workforce is comprised of four distinct generations—Traditionalists, Boomers, Xers, and Millennials. *Ties to Tattoos* suggests ways to recruit, reward, manage, motivate, train, and retain employees within a generationally diverse workplace. Today's workforce brings with it a new set of challenges and opportunities: the looming labor shortage, sagging productivity, knowledge transfer, the language barrier, and stereotypes. *Ties to Tattoos* addresses how best to take advantage of the challenges and the opportunities they create.

The Looming Labor Shortage

For most companies, people are *the* key resource. So let me ask you a couple of questions. First, is your key resource old or young? According to the Bureau of Labor Statistics, the number of older workers is skyrocketing. In fact, from 2000 to 2005, the number of employees fifty-five and older increased nearly 30 percent while the number of twenty-five to fifty-four-year-olds increased just 1 percent. Second, is your key resource expanding or shrinking? As older workers retire, 168 million jobs will open up by 2010. The problem is we have only 158 million younger workers ready to take their place. The issue of scarce resources is critical to your business because the growth and size of your company is limited by its most scarce resource. For most companies, that limiting resource is the scarcity of people, a problem expected to get worse in the near future rather than better.

The Sagging Productivity Picture

The shortage of workers isn't the only looming crisis. An equally important concern is how to boost productivity with the workers you already have. In the past, many performance directives, incentive plans, and human resource policies focused on uniformity. In many ways, this made sense because the workplace of yesteryear was reasonably homogenous. Such uniform company policies employed rigid rules that promised fair and equitable treatment. A case can be made that uniform policies and programs were effective. That was then. Today we no longer work in a uniform environment. We no longer have a Workforce of One. Today's workforce is made up of four generations—Traditionalists (born 1922 to 1943), Boomers (born 1944 to 1960), Xers (born 1961 to 1980), and Millennials (born 1981 to 2000). Now more than ever, people strategies must be flexible and offer options that meet the needs of your workplace demographic.

The Knowledge Transfer Conundrum

As unwelcoming as managing four separate and unique generations may seem, the future looks even bleaker. Over the next dozen years, all but the most die-hard Traditionalists will have left the workforce and taken with them their strong sense of loyalty and sacrifice. Now come the Boomers, 76 million of them, planning their retirements and taking with them a vast reservoir of company knowledge and expertise. How then do you capture this vast knowledge base and share it with the upcoming generations? Or, in practical terms, how do you organize, create, capture, and distribute company knowledge to future users. How do you ensure that conceptual skills, socialization, and other non-explicit types of knowledge gleaned from your company by Boomers over the past twenty years is transmitted, in a way that makes sense, to younger Xers and Millennials?

Knowledge transfer is only half the problem. The other half is creating new communication tools that speak to an entirely new workplace demographic. E-mail, for example, may have been a godsend for Boomers, but to Xers and Millennials, e-mail is the dinosaur of an ever-growing set of revolutionary technology communication tools.

As the last of the Boomers reach retirement, by 2020, the new workforce will be comprised of two entirely new and different demographics—Xers and Millennials.

So, is your company ready for the change? Do you understand the difference between breakthrough strategies for Traditionalists and Boomers and those for Xers and Millennials? Do you have a clear strategy to recruit, reward, manage, motivate, train, and retain this entirely new demographic? And if you think the old "humans as commodities" strategies are good enough, you and your company are destined to fail.

Let's slow down. The year 2020 is a long way off. What's the rush? Why must I, as a company leader, do anything right now? The reason is this: if you don't have a strategy to deal with the radically new workforce of 2020, I guarantee you don't have a strategy to deal with your current workforce. And the current multigenerational workforce is, in many ways, much more complex than the workforce of the future.

The difference between Traditionalists (whose core values are conformity and sacrifice) and Boomers (whose core values are optimism and personal growth) is striking. However, the differences between Traditionalists, Boomers, Xers (whose core values are technoliteracy and informality), and Millennials (whose core values are sociability and street smarts) are complicated by a magnitude of ten.

Where Boomers are optimistic, Xers are reactive. Where Traditionalists preach patience, Xers preach fun. Where Boomers want personal gratification, Millennials want morality. Where Millennials strive for civic duty, Xers strive for self-reliance. The old one-size-fits-all recruiting, rewarding, and managing strategies no longer work. In fact, they haven't worked for some time.

What does work, however, is assessing how these four generational cohorts differ and adjusting your people strategies accordingly. If your company depends on recruiting fresh talent, for example, and what company doesn't, your first step is to identify your target job candidate and learn the language.

The Language Barrier

In searching for Xers, for example, recruiters have learned to avoid the hype. Xers are looking for rock-hard, specific information on job responsibilities and a chance to go global. Xers want to know about money, continual education, and working in the trendy Seattle office versus the dusty satellite office in the Oklahoma panhandle. And they aren't afraid to ask. In other words, Xers respond when you speak in terms they understand: What's In It For Me (WIIFM)?

So what happens if you don't speak the language?

What if you let loose your top recruiter, a Traditionalist so loyal to the company you wish you had a hundred of her, and she's a bit turned off when an Xer asks about family leave, a shot at the office in Geneva, and how long before he can expect his first promotion? A Traditionalist wouldn't dare ask such things on a first interview and finds the questions disrespectful. She doesn't say it, but she's bowled over that a young grad would have the gumption to ask. Not to mention that this particular Xer has a hollow ring the size of a quarter stretching out his ear lobe (called a flesh tunnel, if you're interested) that looks like something you've seen on a *National Geographic* special about primitive tribes of the Amazon.

What happens is the Traditionalist politely answers all the Xers questions, the Xer intuitively knows he hasn't got a chance at the job and isn't all that bent out of shape about it, and everyone walks away, if not exactly happy, at least happy the interview is over. Not speaking the language meant your top recruiter disregarded an otherwise perfectly qualified candidate. And for no other reason than she was irked by an applicant with distinctly different core values and cultural influences than her own, that applicant is now working for your competitor.

Companies like WinStar World Casinos are taking a different approach. Human resource and marketing executives at the company are actively seeking to hire Xers by creating recruiting messages that appeal specifically to this self-reliant and pragmatic cohort. WinStar needed to hire approximately 1,100 new employees for its gaming, hotel, and retail operations throughout the Midwest. One element of the campaign included printing employment and benefit information on the back of playing cards. The playing cards are trendy, casual, and fun. Remember that Xers value informality and fun. In fact, WinStar's slogan on the back of the card says, "At WinStar Casinos, having fun is just a part of the job."

Millennials, on the other hand, speak a different language. When looking for a job, your typical Millennial wants to be the top dog, or at least scrambling up the corporate ladder when they walk in the door. They believe they deserve the position they want, whether experienced or not. Millennials aren't against hard work by any means. In fact, they are tech-savvy multitaskers with a tenacious spirit. This is not a lazy generation, just one that wants and expects immediate gratification. Career advancement is at the top of their priorities, as are promotional opportunities and the chance to make a difference. They aren't focused on doing their own thing. Far from it, Millennials are willing to sacrifice to achieve larger goals.

Millennials are frantic to do something meaningful with their lives. This is a group interested in youth outreach, rebuilding

communities, and telling the mayor what they think of him without embarrassment. They want to be remembered and are enticed by opportunities to do something significant. To speak the Millennials' language, you must let them know they are needed and valued. They can help turn things around. No matter that your job candidate is wearing big rattan sandals and a pink cardigan sweater that shows too much cleavage and bears a tiny tattoo of a bird on her lower neck. Tell her she can be a hero. Money is a minor enticement. Instead, offer her security and career opportunities, upward mobility, and flexibility to work from home when needed.

"Some things don't change," says Jeff Powell, CEO of Razzoo's Cajun Café, a food chain with eleven restaurants throughout the Dallas/Fort Worth area. "Human principles have not changed. People tell me the new generation lacks passion and loyalty, but I think that's bunk. People are just as passionate as they have always been. They will be loyal to true principles. You just have to understand the deal. You may need to use different words to communicate the deal, but so what? That has always been true."

Building Shared Values

Okay, so now you have a handle on some of the challenges. And let's say you even know the generational mix of your organization—say your company mimics the broader American workforce: 10 percent Traditionalists, 45 percent Boomers, 30 percent Xers, and 15 percent Millennials. Now what? Your objective is to design people strategies that make everyone in this 10/45/30/15 split happy. Just imagine a set of strategies that work equally for a few duty-bound Traditionalists, a lot of workaholic Boomers, a few less-tattooed Xers, and a rapidly growing bunch of texting Millennials. What exactly will that set of people strategies look like for your organization?

Before we get ahead of ourselves, let me mention one more challenge. Stereotypes. In this case, I'm referring to treating people a certain way based solely on age. It's wrong. It's counterproductive. And it's going on right now. I mean this very minute. As you read these words, company managers are out in the field or in the office or down on the plant floor putting out fires based exclusively on stereotypes. Xers are railing against Traditionalists for being resistant to change, for being unwilling to hand over the reins. Boomers are begrudging Xers for finding it so easy to change jobs on a whim. Boomers are further miffed that Xers thought to demand balance in their work and personal lives. Traditionalists resent Millennials for their entitlement mentality, especially so when Traditionalists had to work for every penny they earned. Millennials resent Boomers for leaving the planet in a mess. And on it goes. All of this anger and frustration comes to a head at work because each generation is competing for the same scarce resource—a way to earn a living.

The technological revolution has only made generational stereotyping worse. More than any other influence, the use and adaptability to technology has put a greater perceived divide between those who grew up without technology and those born into phones with virtual buttons and GPS mapping and Internet access anywhere anytime.

Even with these daunting challenges ahead of you, innovative companies have found ways to rally the troops. Your first step is to instill a sense of shared unity, define and promote shared goals, and create a culture of purpose. You do these things by establishing inspiring organizational goals, setting priorities for those goals, and sticking to them. Shared goals and values strengthen the critical link between companies, workers, and culture. At the same time, shared goals create a workplace where workers are encouraged and willing to share knowledge. Begin today to promote shared company values and help close the gaps that generational conflicts unintentionally expose. Helping people find meaning and purpose in their work can transcend the challenges of cultural barriers, language, and stereotypes.

The differences between Traditionalists, Boomers, Xers, and Millennials are about more than language, more than age, and more than the latent mistrust of one generation of another. Each group behaves differently, thinks differently, and is motivated differently. Each cohort has different goals, dreams, and desires. Make no mistake, the challenges are real. The opportunities for leveraging these differences are equally real. By shifting focus and zeroing in on the talents and strengths of your workforce, you can boost productivity, minimize conflicts, and create a shared culture of innovation, loyalty, and growth.

Chapter Two

Identifying Your Generational Mix

> "I'm not trying to cause a big sensation, I'm just
> talkin' 'bout my generation."
>
> —The Who

I'm a Boomer. You're an Xer. The patient old guy with the tie, he's a Traditionalist. And the kid wearing flip-flops and listening to the iPod while sending text messages, she's a Millennial. Okay, so the names sound silly. So what? We work in an environment with four distinct generations and each of these generational groups has unique attitudes and goals about work and their role in the workplace. To ignore this fact is tantamount to neglecting the most significant competitive advantage to come along in twenty years.

By way of a short introduction, let me define each generation.

Traditionalists, also known as Veterans, were born between 1922 and 1943 and grew up during the enormous upheavals of depression and war. They are not easily adaptive. They're also risk-averse and conformists.

Baby Boomers were born between 1944 and 1960 and comprise a majority of today's workers. This is the largest generation in human history, with approximately 76 million Boomers in the United States. They are overachievers, idealists, inspired, and often narcissistic.

Generation Xers were born between 1961 and 1980 in vast contrast to prior generations and possibly the least understood of these generations. They value portable careers and are loyal to themselves and not organizations. They are looking for a leader and mentor, not necessarily their boss, and they are very techno-literate.

Millennials, also known as "Generation WHY," or as I like to call them, "Trophy Babies," were born between 1981 and 2000. Mostly children of the Boomers, they are about 76 million strong, nearly as large as their parents' generation. They are multitaskers, confident, and team oriented. This is the generation that has been rewarded for showing up to soccer practice, never mind winning. If you manage a group of this generation, get ready to provide constant daily feedback.

Measuring Values

As a human resources consultant, I don't often receive calls or e-mails from clients complaining about generational issues. Instead, they tell me a story or ask for solutions to problems. In these stories, what I hear is "I'm an Xer manager, and I need to know how to deal with employees who are older than I am." Or "I am a Traditionalist business owner, and we can't seem to retain Millennials." Or "I'm a

Boomer, and I'm afraid I'm going to be replaced by one of the more tech-savvy Xers on my staff." Each of these generational groups holds different values. Traditionalists, the oldest cohort, value patience, delayed reward, and duty before pleasure. Millennials, the youngest cohort, value diversity, morality, and sociability. It's easy to spot a Millennial because he's got his iPhone in his hand while texting a coworker, listening to music via barely noticeable earbuds, and quickly fiddling with the GPS on the same phone in a rush to visit a client—all while driving.

Entire books have been written on each of these generational types. Our focus here isn't to give an encyclopedia of information on Traditionalists, Boomers, Xers, and Millennials, but to give enough information to help you create new programs to recruit, manage, and motivate your workforce. The table below offers an overview of the core values and goals of each generational type.

GENERATIONAL VALUES			
	COVER VALUES	GOALS	HEROES
Traditionalists	Fiscal restraint Work ethic Sacrifice	To be respected To be valued	Superman Joe DiMaggio Barbara Walters
Boomers	Ideals Success Long hours	Lifelong learning	John Glenn Michael Jordan Martin Luther King, Jr.
Xers	Entrepreneurship Ambition Self-trust	Independence No rules	Someone they seek out
Millennials	Technological savvy Eagerness to learn Confidence	A chance at heroism To make a difference	Danica Patrick Jennifer Hudson Josh Groban

Traditionalists value consistency and uniformity. Their spending is conservative, which brings us to the Millennials' technology gadgets. A Traditionalist would no more spend $599 for a phone (the initial cost of Apple's iPhone 8GB model), even if it has three thousand features, than he would buy a fifty-thousand-dollar Rolex. Millennials on the other hand, value movement, achievement, and multitasking. As for the cost of the phone, it's just money, and what is money if not a tool to buy the things they want? And what Millennials want isn't so much cell phones, PDAs, and video conferencing laptops as much as a social connection. They want to be in constant contact with people and information, and they want to make a difference.

Generational value gaps at work are big and getting bigger. The reason is simple. With four generations in the workplace, these groups bring with them four individual persona determined by common age, common beliefs and behaviors, and a perceived generational membership. In other words, Xers choose to see themselves as belonging to the Xer generation. Boomers to the Boomer generation, and so on. And in the process, the workplace has become inundated with generational strife. And to make it even more confusing, how about those of us who were born at the end of the range of a specific generation and can truly identify with the next generation? The Generational Personality is then of the next generational personality, such as mine . . . I am an Xer by age but a Boomer in lifestyle and personality.

Multigenerational clashes are routine and increasing at an alarming rate. Worse, most organizations are not doing anything about it. Instead, many companies are addressing the problems piecemeal, often entirely misdiagnosing the root causes and firing employees or, at a minimum, transferring employees to another department and hoping for the best. For example, repeated conflicts between a thirty-year-old Xer managing a sixty-five-year-old Traditionalist are often written off as a personal conflict rather than what they likely are, which is a conflict in values and cultural influences. Resolving these conflicts isn't easy because cultural influences can't be reversed, ever, and it can take years to change a person's values, assuming an employee wanted to change. In other words, these types of conflicts will continue to occur until companies and senior management teams recognize them as a clash of generational values and address them as such.

These types of value clashes are widespread. A fifty-year-old Boomer routinely scolds a twenty-two-year-old Millennial for wearing low-cut pants that show off his or her underwear. Or a sixty-seven-year-old Traditionalist and war veteran refuses to sit next to a twenty-year-old Millennial because she has a habit of twirling the silver stud in her upper lip whenever she is on the phone with a client. The Traditionalist, a top performing salesman, sees the lip stud as disrespectful. The Millennial, also a top performer, thinks the stud is attractive, or she did until her coworker started sounding off. Far from becoming argumentative over the complaints, she's hurt and goes to the bathroom to cry. The director of regional sales, a forty-nine-year-old Boomer, is fed up and ready to fire both of them.

The solution to workplace conflicts like these isn't firing staff who complain and it is not transferring employees to different managers. It isn't implementing policies that force everyone into a single innocuous mold. The answer is in understanding these conflicts for what they are: generational differences based on the core values that each generation holds to be meaningful and true. Differences that won't change after one good talking to, or a new policy, or a new seating chart, or even a new organizational chart. The solution is to understand your company's generational mix, to assess the values of the groups within that mix, to listen to each generation's needs and motivations, and to implement programs, processes, and policies that make the best use of the talent within your organization.

Adding Up the Voices

"Most HR departments are built on an old model," says Lin O'Neill, president of Futures Consulting. Sticky people issues can be the result of a wide range of factors. One factor is that companies don't often listen to employees. Or, they don't have mechanisms to gather feedback from employees. The real question is: what do your employees want? Before you can design the appropriate people strategy, it's critical to know what motivates your workforce. Do your employees want clear goals and respect (Traditionalists), big dollars and learning opportunities (Boomers), access to new technology and flexible hours and an informal work environment (Xers), timely information and lots of it (Millennials), or a host of other wants and needs that apply to all workers including a sense of purpose, trust, interesting work, appreciation, a good boss, and compatible coworkers?

If you don't have a strategy to communicate with employees and, within that strategy, several practical programs to solicit, gather, and store employee feedback, then you are simply guessing at what drives your people, or worse, you are assuming what drives you as the CEO or senior executive will drive them. And if you are a Boomer working in an industry where most of your workers are Xers or Millennials, for example, you couldn't be more wrong.

The key to taking advantage of your multigenerational workforce is understanding the underlying needs driving your people, learning to appreciate those different needs, and creating processes that are responsive and effective. Some companies believe the processes they have in place are doing a fine job for communicating with employees. The question becomes: "Compared to what?" At a recent conference, Lin O'Neill spoke to a senior-level human resource manager, let's call her Sue, who worked for a large multinational corporation. Sue mentioned the tools her company used to communicate with and get feedback from employees.

"Like what?" Lin asked.

"Oh, lots of things," Sue said.

"Are you setting up a Wiki for your employees to contribute?"

"Well, no. Not exactly."

"Internal blogs for employees to post concerns about job issues?"

"No, not blogs."

"Are you using internal broadcast systems, virtual conversations, that sort of thing?"

"I don't think so," Sue said.

"How about access to multimedia like music, video, and photos for cell phones and PDAs? I know of companies sending video clips of training sessions to employees."

Sue rooted around in her briefcase. "Let me get a piece of paper. I need to write this down." Lin and Sue stood in the center of a wide lobby. Conference-goers chatted in small groups all around them. Sue found a pen and paper. "What else?"

"If you mean how do you open a dialogue with your employees, there are several ways. How about downloadable podcasts of lectures, annual stockholders meetings, or comments by senior management; archived video conferences of key meetings, especially those that address new initiatives, changes in company vision, new products, and acquisitions; or wireless workforce networks to share information that will appeal to your tech-savvy employees? Some companies create communications steering committees that then develop clear communication policies. The possibilities are, well, I don't know about endless, but there are a lot of them."

"That's it?"

"How about creating your own internal social networking site? Or you can create a company profile on an existing site like Bebo and MySpace and Facebook. Pepsi created a beautiful company profile on MySpace for its purified water brand Aquafina."

Sue scribbled on a piece of paper. "It's overwhelming, isn't it?"

"No, not really," Lin said. "It's simply a matter of deciding what works best for your employees and your objectives."

"If you had to choose just one way to connect with employees, which would you choose?"

"First, if the goal is to talk to your employees, you use one set of tools. If the goal is to listen to your employees, you use another set of tools. In either case, you use the tools that make the most sense to your employees. If your staff is mostly Boomers, e-mail, e-newsletters, and a company intranet might be fine. If you employ a majority of Millennials, you'll need to use wireless technologies that can communicate with laptops, PDAs, and the latest phones. E-mail is a no-brainer, but I'd add instant messaging, text messaging, streaming video, podcasts, RSS feeds, social networking, and blogs."

Sue frowned. She stared at a group of people shuffling back into the conference room.

Lin said, "Tell me again how your company communicates with employees."

"E-mail, I guess."

"I mean how do you know what your employees think and feel?"

"We have a telephone hotline," Sue said.

"And people actually use it?"

"No, not really. Or, rather, it's hard to tell because it usually goes unanswered."

"Annual surveys?"

"No."

"If you don't mind me saying, it sounds a bit '80s."

"Yeah, I guess it does."

Don't let this happen to you. Communicating with employees has always been important. But within the new multigenerational workplace, it's essential. Communication works both ways. The easiest fix is for you to communicate with your employees. This approach is one way, from company to employer, and whatever method you choose—face-to-face meetings, e-mail, video, podcasts, blogs, social media, etc.—it is important you do it now and do it regularly. For some segment of your workforce, just receiving this information satisfies a key need because you care enough to keep them informed. Still others will want a two-way communication channel, a way for workers to respond to the company. Many employees, if given an appropriate channel, will give you plenty of feedback on their job, fellow employees, bosses, company operations, marketing, strategy, clients, and a host of other information that will help you, as a senior manager, stay up-to-date on the issues affecting your people.

What Is Your Generational Mix?

At your next family reunion or holiday gathering, look around at the generations present. Who has an iPod in his pocket, ready at the first sign of boredom to connect outside the group? Who is sitting at the head of the table telling stories about the family's past? Who is eager to get the serving and eating done quickly and move through the planned family bonding to get on the road and meet the day's schedule? Who looks out of place with a nose ring and tattoos?

If your family is like mine, you can identify four generational personalities seated around the table. The number of Traditionalists, Boomers, Xers, and Millennials contributes to the flavor of the conversation and the family dynamic. If you are the host, likely you took into account the percentage of each and the blend of types and interests as you planned the festivities. If you did not, probably three of the four will tune out after dessert.

This same process works in your company as you identify the generational mix—the percent or ratio of Traditionalists, Boomers, Xers, and Millennials within your organization. The most effortless method is a simple head count. Look up each employee's birth date, and place the employee into one of the four categories based on age. It sounds easy and it is. The problem is that not all Traditionalists, for example, share consistent traits. Some might really think, act, and respond like a Boomer, or even an Xer. Not every Traditionalist will value the same things as the Traditionalist who may have been raised in a home with better financial support during the Depression and did not suffer the same sacrifices. The objective here isn't to create people strategies based on well-defined age brackets or to demand that employees conform to their peers based on a common age. The goal is to boost company productivity and minimize time-wasting generational conflicts by better understanding your workforce, their generational personalities, and the messages that motivate each group.

Knowing how many seventy-year-olds your company employs, for example, relative to twenty-five-year-olds is valuable. However, it isn't as valuable as knowing how much of your workforce considers itself adaptive (Traditionalist), idealistic (Boomer), reactive (Xer), or civic minded (Millennial). In other words, it is more useful to know how employees see themselves and how they will behave than how old they are.

Another approach to identifying the generations is to use a personality test. Such a test can quickly identify generational influences, ideals, cultural norms, and work habits. The test can also outline organization and management styles from a generational perspective.

There is yet another way to think about understanding your company makeup. How about this: do your employees identify with Harry Belafonte or LeAnn Rimes, Dorothy Hamill or Tara Lipinski, Lee Iacocca or Michael Dell, swing or SKA, Ella Fitzgerald or Bon Jovi? As a leader, young or old, just because you don't know the names mentioned above doesn't mean your employees don't.

To remain competitive in a multigenerational work environment requires that you and your top management team have at least a basic understanding of your employee preferences, goals, hobbies, and workplace drivers before you can create effective people strategies. This understanding allows you to implement programs and procedures that proactively address the changing workforce over the next fifteen years, develop a perspective to understand the differences generations bring to your products and services, and recognize the impact of current organizational practices and management styles on newer generations of workers.

Recognizing a Traditionalist

Generational differences are not going away. In fact, as the generations age, they won't become more alike, but rather their generational personalities will likely grow stronger throughout their lives. Indeed, when hard times hit, each generation is likely to entrench themselves into old habits and ingrained attitudes and behaviors. Now might be a good time to examine each generation individually to study the events and conditions during those formative years and to visualize the point of view through which each generation sees the world. The table below offers an overview of generational influences.

GENERATIONAL INFLUENCES			
	KEY EVENTS	POP CULTURE	WHAT THEY READ
Traditionalists	Cuban Missile Crisis Pearl Harbor Korean War	Wheaties Mickey Mouse *The Lone Ranger*	Daily newspaper Bible *Gone with the Wind*
Boomers	Rosa Parks Civil Rights Act M.L. King, Jr. assassination Vietnam War	Slinkies TV dinners The peace sign	*Atlas Shrugged* *Catcher in the Rye* *Lord of the Rings*
Xers	John Lennon shot *Challenger* disaster Exxon Valdez oil spill	Brady Bunch E.T. Cabbage Patch Kids	*The Stand* *Angels and Demons* *Wired* magazine
Millennials	Oklahoma City bombings Clinton/Lewinsky Columbine H.S. massacre	Barney Oprah X Games	*Harry Potter* Prefer video games

Elders first. Traditionalists came of age during the Great Depression and World War II. This generation had plenty of hard times. Material goods were scarce, and they were typically the millionaire's next door. The need to save for a rainy day was tangible, and "waste not, want not" was closer to a commandment than a slogan. The personality of a true Traditionalist can best be described as loyal. They are respectful to the law, true to family and friends, unswerving in allegiance. This generation learned at an early age that by putting aside the needs and wants of the individual and working together toward common goals they could accomplish amazing feats. This generation still has an immense amount of faith in institutions—church, government, and military.

When they entered the workforce, Traditionalists expected to build a lifetime career with a single employer. At a minimum, they expected to work in a single industry. That loyalty combined with the desire to leave a lasting legacy has guided Traditionalists in planning their careers. It is critical to recognize the deep sense of personal responsibility felt by many Traditionalists toward their employer. Rather than thinking of Traditionalists as over-the-hill, (and let's face it, many are in their seventies and eighties), it is more helpful to see them as moving along a path that involves service, loyalty, and the desire to give to their communities. Smart companies are inviting Traditionalists to retool their careers into roles as leaders, mentors, consultants, and trainers—positions that allow them to retool themselves and leverage a lifetime of experience to add to their legacy.

Pinpointing a Boomer

Seventy-six million Boomers have changed every market they entered, from the supermarket to the job market to the stock market. Ask Boomers about the greatest invention of their childhood and they will tell you television. And with the introduction of television, the generation gap between Boomers and Traditionalists gradually widened. Boomers were the first generation of TV addicts. They were influenced by wholesome shows like *The Adventures of Ozzie and Harriet, I Love Lucy, Leave It to Beaver,* and *The Lone Ranger*—All shows unknown to their parents. As Boomers grew up, they believed in their own optimism and really did think that they could change the world. If the key word to remember about Traditionalists is "loyal," the key word for Boomers is "optimistic." They entered the workforce believing they could do anything and become anything, and they have.

Boomers want to excel in their careers. As this group approaches retirement, they realize they have limited time to stand out and earn at peak capacity, and they want to make the most of these remaining career years in the workforce. While Boomers aren't likely to job-hop, employers can't assume that Boomers will wait forever for top positions and the corner office to open up. As millions of Boomers age, now is the time for organizations to consider how they will seize Boomer loyalty and optimism. This generation loves to be challenged. They crave opportunities that will vault them to the next level in terms of opportunity, visibility, or challenge.

Baby Boomers are also questioning their career choices, wondering if they have meaning. One of my dearest friends, a Boomer, has been a highly successful independent insurance broker for more than twenty years. Recently she decided that her work no longer personally fulfilled her, and she has begun looking at the next ten years of her work life, asking herself, "What do I want? What will give me joy? Will it make an impact on my community?" With regard to this kind of late-career soul-searching, she isn't alone.

Boomers are searching for meaning. Those with the financial means aren't afraid to move from one career to another to find that meaning. In some ways, "meaning" translates to the notion of giving back. And to fulfill this need to give back, Boomers support social, environmental, or charitable programs and encourage their employees to do the same. The point here is that Boomers want to make a difference, and they look for employers with the same commitment. Boomers are strategic thinkers. Their technical knowledge, job skills, and experience give them the unique ability to visualize the big picture in terms of organizational vision, strategies, and tactics. This buildup of wisdom, passion, and do-it-now attitude makes Boomers ideal employees. Companies that tap into this career intensity will be rewarded.

Spotting an Xer

Xers are possibly the most misunderstood generation in the workforce today. This growing influential generation has worked to carve out its own identity separate from the Boomers and Traditionalists. Early on, Xers were the "show me the money" generation, because they knew how to negotiate and ask for what they wanted! They demanded and in many cases received high salaries in trade for their tech savvy. At the same time, Xers watched company leaders indicted for billions of dollars in improper bookkeeping, accounting fraud, embezzlement, inflating subscriber numbers, evading taxes, recommending questionable stocks, and posting misleading audit reports. Company executives at Enron, Arthur Andersen, WorldCom, Adelphia, Tyco, Rite Aid, Merrill Lynch, Waste Management, Cendant Corp., and others were exposed as cheats. Far from heroes, these icons of industry were petty moneygrubbers.

As a result, Xers are skeptics. They grew up watching American institutions called into question. From the presidency to the military to organized religion to corporate America, you name the institution, and Xers can name the crime.

Xers want "portable" careers. Forget job security. Xers long for career security and are building a repertoire of skills and experiences they can take with them from job to job. In interviews, Xers tell me they can't stand the thought of reaching a dead-end career at the same company with only a plaque waiting for them. To cynical Xers, everything is temporary. Companies are bought and sold daily. Chief executive officers and executive managers swap jobs as often as pro athletes swap teams. Technology is changing at a mind-numbing rate. Computer and cell phone technology becomes obsolete in a matter of months, weeks, and even days. With this momentum of change swirling around their heads, Xers can't help but constantly reevaluate their career shelf life. It isn't unusual for a Xer to tell me in an interview, "I felt I had to move. I just didn't have enough experience on my resume yet to feel secure." It's easy to see why Boomers and Traditionalists often describe Xers as flaky and disloyal. One thirty-year-old I interviewed said she left her job where she was adored because she was not progressing quickly enough. This was after only two years at the company.

Xers want career security. But that doesn't mean they can't find that security within a single organization, within your organization, if you can offer benefits and new opportunities that Xers want. To keep Xers on the job, organizations must maintain a running dialogue about career goals—where the employee is going and what skills and accomplishments are going to get them there. If Xers feel they are being coached, trained, and genuinely building a career portfolio, they are much more likely to stay.

For Xers, career-path time horizons are shrinking. Xers are constantly pulling out their career maps to double-check their direction and, if required, to make a detour. Ask your Xer employees to share the map with you. This simple act of asking has several benefits for an employer. Asking for the map shows that you understand how Xers think. You understand that Xers aren't a permanent fixture in your employee pool and will remain only as long as they are improving their skills. Asking for the map shows you care. Asking for the map is a tangible example of an employer listening to employees.

Besides, if you don't ask to see an employee's career map, a competitor will.

Talk to your Xer staff about career paths, and do it now. During the initial job interviews, don't be astonished if Xers ask detailed questions about career potential. To appeal to Xers, you must give them a glimpse of the future. On day-one orientation meetings, talk about the employee and his career. Talk about the threshold for promotions, lateral transfers, and positions in exciting and remote, if not exotic, locations. Xers want to know where they are going, not five years from now, not in a year, but next month.

One disgruntled Xer called me and said he really loved his job but wasn't sure if he would stick around. As much as he enjoyed his current duties, it wasn't clear where his skills could take him. He didn't understand his career path, nor the advancement track, nor his growth potential within the organization in general. This is a lack of communication that falls squarely on the employer. A new employee may not be happy with the career track, but there is little excuse for not ensuring that all employees know what that career track is. The employee told me that without a feel for his future, just sticking around made him nervous. When I called my client to discuss the employee, I was told he'd only been on the job for six weeks. There is a moral to this story, and it's easy to think the moral might be: Xers are flakes. Or Xers have super-short attention spans. Or even, Xers have fantastically unrealistic career objectives.

I choose to see the story as a cautionary tale for employers.

Recruiting, hiring, and training is expensive. Losing new employees is expensive, wasteful, and time-consuming, not to mention the emotional drain on the entire organization of high employee turnover. This situation and others like it could have been avoided by taking each employee aside and talking through available career options, by involving the employee in thinking through alternatives for advancement, learning, and growth. What if what an employee really wanted wasn't a promotion but a challenge? What if you offered employees a chance to move forward instead of up? What if you had career options that supported several viable alternatives within the organization? What if you could show each employee a future for themselves while laying out the realities of the organization? Do that and you will retain Xers, reduce turnover, and save heaps of money in your recruiting, hiring, and training budgets.

Distinguising a Millennial

The Millennial generation has been called Generation WHY, Baby Busters, Echo Boom, Generation Next, and Nexters. It doesn't matter what you call them. This group of teens and twenty-somethings is 76 million strong and just now flooding the workforce. Millennials are young, confident, sociable, and moral. By moral, I mean they are capable of distinguishing right from wrong and taking a stand. And that stand is not always the position you might expect. Only a day after the Iraq War officially began in March 20, 2003, Ian R. Williams reported on Salon.com that Millennials confounded sociologists by advocating war. "In February 2003, a Gallup Poll reported that 58 percent of teens (Millennials) favored the war (for boys, that number jumped to 66 percent, the same as the population as a whole)." The results are counterintuitive in that we typically think of young people as opposing war.

Millennials are tech-savvy in ways that make Xers and Boomers look like fossils. Millennials love the latest techie gadgets—3G phones, GPS mapping, hands-free everything, voice recognition, portable media players, underwater music players, e-books, high definition camcorders, I could go on and on.

Millennials are loyal. They have faith in institutions. They are optimistic. They are cautious. Millennials have combined these traits into an identity uniquely their own. Think Millennials and the key word is realistic.

The challenge of meeting the needs of this diverse generation cannot be oversimplified. Meeting these needs calls for flexible and perceptive leaders with equally flexible people policies. Millennials understand the importance of balancing hobbies, sports, and volunteer activities with work. Where Traditionalists seek lifetime careers, Boomers stellar careers, and Xers portable careers, Millennials strive for parallel careers. Futurists predict that Millennials will experience as many as ten career changes in their lifetimes. And it's likely that Millennials will reject the Xers distrust of organizations and instead may envision a lifetime career with one company if they can attach themselves to organizations that offer the right combination of challenge, opportunity, and security.

Millennials are capable of learning several jobs simultaneously and performing them equally well. In a tight labor market, relying on Millennials to cover more than one position is a smart strategy. They thrive on multitasking, and putting these abilities to use rather than hiring more employees is cost-effective. Cross-training is a strategy that will appeal to Millennials and help reduce turnover.

This generation is exceptionally talented and has the ability to take on the world, but they are going to ask why first. They will challenge you to rethink the way you have always done things, and if you can open your mind to new processes and procedures, perhaps you will learn something.

Surveying the Troops

In terms of career development, what do your employees want? It's a trick question, because first you have to know what each of your four generational groups want. One answer does not fit all. We know from experience that generational wants are different. If you don't know, then it's time to ask. Surveys are a cheap and effective tool to take the pulse of your workplace.

A recent global survey conducted by BlessingWhite Consulting in 2006 of nearly one thousand executives, managers, and employees revealed that workers don't believe management is supporting their career paths. Of those surveyed, 41 percent said their employer's career development offerings failed to meet their needs. Even the most struggling of companies understands the value of a clearly defined career education and development program. Many of the companies surveyed had career development programs in place. Why then the disconnect between the company believing they have an effective education and development program and the employee's response that the program doesn't address their needs, or worse, that the employee isn't aware the program even exists?

Perhaps the answer is that companies tend to offer a one-size-fits-all solution. A management-training program designed for Traditionalists, for example, won't work for Millennials. Corporate training for Boomers won't appeal to Xers. We can think of these groups as distinctly different sets of career education consumers. Designing programs that appeal to each consumer group becomes important.

Another nagging issue is the age and relevance of your career development program. If your corporate education and training program was designed and put in place five or ten years ago, your workplace mix has likely shifted in the intervening years, making your program irrelevant and next to useless to Xers and Millennials. Boomers, for instance, may have loved the program years ago, but now that your workforce is composed primarily of Xers, the training approach looks antiquated and just plain unappealing. The solution, of course, is to create and offer career development options that specifically address your changing workforce.

To understand what your employees want from the workplace, you must ask and ask often. What staffers wanted from their jobs five years ago, last year, and last month may not be what they want today. In survey after survey, we see a strong disconnect between what managers and senior management thinks their workforce wants and what employees actually want. Employees are often asked to rank high wages, job security, promotions, interesting work, discipline, appreciation, and so on. Managers expect to see high wages and job security at the top of the list. Wrong. Today's workforce wants appreciation and to be kept in the loop—two items that require little if any capital to implement yet can offer a huge boost in overall job satisfaction to employees.

Exactly how you show that appreciation and how you keep Traditionalists, Boomers, Xers, and Millennials informed is another matter. The first step is to gain a better understanding of what your employees really want at work. If you don't know, now is a good time to ask.

. . . a sick feeling came over Hank as he
remembered NOT hiring the newly-elected
Executive of the Year six months earlier
because of his nose ring and funny purple hair.

Chapter Three

Recruiting for a Competitive Advantage

"I like the challenge that recruitment brings.
It's the adrenaline. If your hair's on fire, you're happy."

—Nan Richards, Director of Recruitment
HCA Healthcare

Recruiting for value doesn't have to be difficult. "Value" refers to the boost in long-term performance to your organization by focusing your recruiting efforts on multigenerational diversity as a competitive advantage. At its simplest, the recruiting process consists of four components: understanding exactly what talent your organization and managers need, finding the best sources, attracting the highest quality candidates, and hiring top talent and tracking their success.

Before we jump into specific generational recruiting tactics, let's look at the big picture and the two issues driving recruitment needs at a national and global level—the looming labor shortage and the growth of free agents.

Where Has Everybody Gone?

Over the next two decades, US companies will lose 76 million Boomers to retirement. To fill this void, unskilled Xers and Millennials are waiting patiently in the wings. Even if this mammoth transition goes smoothly, the United States will have approximately an extra thirty million jobs still to be filled. Filling seats is a monumental challenge, but the greater challenge is finding a way to prevent all that job knowledge from slipping out the door. As Boomers retire, they will take with them skills and specific job know-how that has taken decades to accumulate. The resulting job amnesia is compounded by the communication gap between Traditionalists and Boomers and younger generations like Xers and Millennials. There are several broad strategies to address organizational knowledge transfer and none of them are easy. Strategies include encouraging later retirement, outsourcing and free agency employment, mentorships, and succession planning.

What else can you and your organization do?

A good first step is to consider the true effects of a Boomer exodus on your organization. Try starting a committee or strategy group to brainstorm on critical issues and solutions. Initially, you might task the strategy group with responding to some key what-ifs.

- What if we don't have a mechanism to identify, document, and retain knowledge and experience before elder workers leave?

- What if we did have programs to capture key competencies and critical work knowledge? What would those programs cost, and what would they look like?
- What if we encouraged later retirement?
- What if employees took us up on our offer and retired later? Are we positioned to meet the needs of over–sixty-five employees?
- What if our older and younger groups have different learning needs? What are those needs, and how do we best implement processes to respond?
- What if our organization needs to increase its reliance on new immigrants? Where do we find them? How do we recruit them?

Companies and staffing firms in some job markets are already reporting a tightened labor market. In some cities, job vacancies are sitting unfilled for lack of qualified talent. This workforce shortage, combined with an aging workforce, isn't confined to the United States. In Europe and Japan, populations are aging faster than the United States, and by 2025, the number of people between the ages of fifteen and sixty-four is expected to drop significantly. In addition, 86 percent of adults in France quit work by age sixty. In Italy 62 percent call it quits at fifty-five. This dramatic change in global demographics is having a profound impact on future labor supply.

Meanwhile, one of the greatest complaints from global businesses is the lack of highly skilled "C-level" talent: CEOs, CFOs, COOs, and CIOs. In Australia, a survey conducted in May 2006 of over three thousand senior executives found that 78 percent of companies had trouble identifying suitable candidates for leadership positions. In addition, 37 percent of organizations said that identifying future leaders from their internal workforce was a major weakness.

To make matters worse, as technology and the Internet improve our ability to connect remote workers, talented individuals will be able to work from their home country versus being "forced" to stay in or come to the United States for work opportunities. The United States will lose out on a portion of the international labor source we now enjoy. It costs a great deal to sponsor an employee from another country and pay all the immigration fees, but many organizations don't have a choice. They hire talent from India or Brazil or Malaysia and pay to bring key staff to the United States. Another good indicator of how tight the labor market has become is that many recruiting companies now demand automatic retainer fees. Traditionally, recruiting companies got paid if they delivered the successful candidate for a position. But now many recruiters charge for their services whether they fill the position or not, due to the lack of skilled professionals.

The Growth of Free Agency

A new employment mindset is emerging—the rise of the "free agents." These are individuals who freelance and include contract employment, independent consultants, and business-owning entrepreneurs. For some segment of the working population, traditional work arrangements don't work. For these individuals, the old nine-to-five mindset stifles innovation and encourages long-time employees to do nothing. Talented employees are breaking free from that tradition and declaring their independence. Free agents span all ages, professions, incomes, and educational levels. By most estimates, 25 to 30 percent of the nation's workforce is now working as a free agent.

Today's free agent is someone who chooses to work untethered from a large organization. Free agents are choosing their own work paths, choosing the clients they want to work with, and selecting the projects they want to work on. They are reserving the right to say no. Their values differ from a traditional worker. Free agents prioritize freedom and flexibility over the need for security. They are autonomous workers driven by self-gratification and are confident in their ability to market themselves and manage their own careers.

Free agents are interested in expanding their skills, expertise, and personal development. They may choose nonconventional career paths as they are less concerned with climbing a ladder than in building a set of skills and finding a more equitable work-life balance. Surprisingly, more than half of all free agents would not consider returning to a traditional work model. They are happy where they are and confident this work-life model will serve them well. In fact, more than 60 percent of free agents think they make the same or more money than they would in a traditional employment model.

Maybe most surprising is that 88 percent believe demand for their marketable skills is high, a number that surpasses confidence levels of today's traditional workers. Although free agents have not been recognized as a collective force like unions, free agents have long been a large component of the workforce. Temporary staffing companies have made a business of understanding a client's need for free agents as a supplemental workforce for decades.

From a business perspective, the growth of free agents can be attributed to many factors, including downsizing, the pace of innovation, shorter job cycles, globalization, technology, and growth in project work.

Some employment experts predict that free agents will account for 40 percent of the workforce by the year 2014. Surprisingly, free agents already outnumber all the Americans who work for federal, state, and local governments combined. Free agents may be the single largest cluster of workers in the American economy.

Let's be clear. There are times that free agency is not the best choice for most employers. Why? Because potential employees have a choice—work for you and your organization or work for themselves.

So what do employees want?

"First," says Paul Wills, senior vice president of Recruitment Services for Michaels Wilder, Inc., a talent management company, "Potential employees don't want to hear from senior executives, they want to hear from each other why they should work for a company." Wills was retained by my company, Optimance Workforce Strategies, to partner with us to manage a large recruiting project for WinStar World Casinos with the Chickasaw Nation Division of Commerce. His first task was to reverse the typical recruiting paradigm. Rather than senior executives sitting around a boardroom with paper and pencil listing the benefits of working for WinStar, in effect, telling job candidates why they should perform jobs it's likely the senior execs never performed themselves, Wills interviewed focus groups of current employees and asked, "What's so great about working here?"

What he found was that current employees liked working at WinStar because it was a fun and fast-paced environment. For jobs like blackjack dealers, bingo concessions, game techs, bartenders, chefs, and sports writers, the job was anything but boring. Many saw the casino as a career. Employees could succeed and be as aggressive as they wanted in that succession.

Potential employees don't want to hear from the boss. They what to hear from people like themselves. For most jobs, Wills was trying to attract candidates twenty-one to thirty years old. Yet what he found was that WinStar is also a great place for seniors. The challenge was to design multiple recruiting messages that appealed to each target group. Millennials and Xers want fun. Traditionalists want benefits and security.

According to Wills, "What tends to happen in a lot of recruitment efforts is organizations create one message for all comers. Pick a Web site," he says, "and it doesn't matter if you're trying to hire generationally or hire hard-to-fill positions, dealers, nurses, engineers, or any other group, the advertising and recruiting message tends to speak in one voice. And it doesn't matter if you're eighteen or eighty." The problem with one recruiting voice and one message is that it doesn't work.

Recruiters must tailor the message or messages to each of your target groups. Younger generations want fun and don't want to work an eighty-hour work week to get it. For older folks, working at the casino is a great way to make good money. The gaming industry offers benefits, it's secure, and it's a growth industry. It's not going away. The message for younger worker is that WinStar is a fun, hip place to work. For older workers, the message is that WinStar offers good pay, benefits, and loads of security. One job description with two different recruiting messages aimed at two different worker populations has the best chance of attracting the right employee mix.

Job candidates have choices. Those choices can be between free agency, competing companies that recruit with a single voice for all jobs to all candidates, and more-aware organizations that create targeted recruiting and advertising messages that appeal to each generation.

The US Department of Labor estimates that between 8.5 and 30 million people identify themselves as free agents. Xers and Millennials especially value flexibility, informality, and diversity. Given a choice, Xers and Millennials may opt for free agency for the flexibility alone. If your company can't offer a work environment that supports these values, you're potential labor pool is even smaller than you expected.

Rethinking Free Agency

If what job candidates really want is to be a free agent, then why fight it? All this talk of competing with free agents may be the wrong approach for your organization. It's possible that to grow your business, cut costs, improve customer service, boost innovation, and be as nimble as your organization can be, free agency may be just the answer to your recruiting objectives. Today most Fortune 500 companies couldn't function without free agents, nor could pharmaceutical companies, law firms, and hospitals. Some industries have little choice but to embrace the free agent trend.

Free agency can help innovative companies compete by shifting the employer/employee paradigm from a goal of employment to one of employability. For employers, this means understanding the needs of your workforce, identifying the skills you need for specific projects and processes, and developing recruiting and hiring models that support a mobile workforce.

If we set aside the question of how to compete with free agency, a more helpful question is, how do you tailor your organization to promote free agency? How do you make free agency work for you as a sustainable competitive advantage? The answer is to create an environment where part-time and short-term workers are valued and viewed as critical and necessary contributors. Celebrate the accomplishments of your flexible workers and build programs that ensure free agents are deeply connected to your mission and know they are a vital part of the corporate community.

eWomenNetwork Inc., a resource for connecting and promoting women and their businesses, successfully uses free agents for marketing, publicity, writing, and technical support. These contract workers are as connected to the company as the employees. They are invited to parties, asked to attend training events and participate in sales meetings, and are routinely co-opted for committees. Free agents and full-time employees are treated differently in only one aspect—how they get paid. A free agent's invoice is processed through the accounting department instead of the payroll department. Regardless of how free agents are paid, they are on the team, just like everyone else. And most important, they know their contributions are valued.

While Xers and Millennials have an intuitive bond to flexible work environments, it's Boomers who have the skills and experience to make free agency worthwhile. Boomers lead the trend of workers morphing into free agents, and as Boomers leave your organization, it is critical to have a process to gather future contact information and create a mechanism to stay in touch. Make sure departing employees know the door is open to future contract employment. In doing so, you have a good chance of connecting with this knowledge if and when you need it. Skip this step and you're likely to end up with a gaping hole in your management knowledge base.

I'm not suggesting that most of your company's employees should be free agents. I'm also not suggesting that you outsource large pieces of your business just because you can. I am suggesting that you identify those areas or functions that could benefit from special expertise and then fill in that expertise with short-term or contract help.

Jeff B. Powell, President of Razzoo's Cajun Café, did just that. Razzoo's Cajun Café opened in 1995 and has since grown into an eleven-unit, casual-dining chain, based in Addison, Texas. Powell says, "You outsource transactions. You outsource tactical work. We outsource payroll, for instance. It's a transaction. Some businesses outsource call centers." For anything that has to do with strategic applications, Powell's strategy is not to outsource, but to "co-source." A co-source is a strategic partner, a team of individuals who have the ability and expertise to fill the voids within the organization. It's a close relationship that goes well beyond the "stay out of trouble" outsourcing of compliance tasks like training, quality control, legal, and some human resource functions. "Co-sourcing has a lot to do with management development," says Powell. "It's about getting to know the whole organization and developing the confidential support and one-on-one relationship."

Powell made the decision to co-source HR and recruiting functions because the HR team he inherited at Razzoo's wasn't qualified to handle the company's growth. "I had limited time to mentor a new HR executive," he says. "But I needed that fifteen or twenty-year, broad perspective and experience that I really didn't have the time to develop. I didn't think I'd be doing somebody a service by bringing them in-house, because I didn't know where they'd get their development. It just made a ton of sense to do it this way."

Managing free agents and contract labor brings its own set of challenges. The two most pressing challenges are social security benefits and health care.

The Social Security Administration has in place regulations that apply to workers who qualify for partial social security benefits. Most applicants have a choice to collect partial social benefits beginning at age sixty-two or wait to collect full benefits at sixty-five to sixty-seven depending on your date of birth. For those collecting early benefits, the Social Security Administration limits how much recipients can earn without paying a penalty. For instance, my parents were born in 1942 and 1943 and are able to earn $12,960. Earn more than that and one of every two dollars of social security benefit is deducted. What this means is that both employers and free agents need an accurate process to monitor annual earnings.

One approach to the social security dilemma, at least at the national level, is to stretch the retirement age. The United

Kingdom recently implemented legislation that increased the retirement age from sixty-five to sixty-eight. In a similar move, the US legislation raised the early retirement age from sixty-two to sixty-seven, effective 2027. Other countries are taking a more aggressive approach. The German government, for instance, has worked with worker unions since 2005 in an effort to promote senior employment. The German Federal Ministry of Labour and Social Affairs has spent $250 million Euros to launch "Initiative 50 Plus," an employment program to put one hundred thousand seniors to work over the next three years.

The number two pressing issue to free agency is health care. Free agents simply don't have access to affordable health care benefits. Kelly Services, Inc., the temporary staffing agency, provides a good example of the magnitude of the problem. Kelly employs approximately 150,000 employees on a daily basis, 700,000 annually. 70 percent of Kelly's employees work for less than two months, 50 percent work less than one month, and 30 percent work for about a week. Most health care coverage requires a thirty-day waiting period before the policy becomes effective. A sixty-day wait is not uncommon. The waiting period makes it virtually impossible for Kelly to provide health insurance for a majority of its employees.

The bottom line is that health care reform is badly needed and companies that come up with strategies to offer health benefits to their free agent labor pool will have a strategic advantage in attracting and retaining key talent.

Attracting Millennials

The Millennial worker is perfectly in sync with the free agent mentality. They expect to build a set of skills for lifetime employability rather than lifetime employment. If they cannot find an organization to offer those skills, they'll put themselves up for sale, just like any other commodity. They'll expect, not just hope, to make a difference. They are mobile and supremely flexible. They prioritize their life when making career decisions. They take responsibility for their own careers. And they define wealth in entirely new ways.

A hundred years ago, wealth was defined in terms of how much land you owned. Along came the industrial revolution and the definition of wealth changed—it now meant money. Today's wealth is viewed in terms of information and knowledge. The more knowledge you have, the wealthier you are. In a land-based economy, if I gave you half my land, I no longer have the land. If I give you half my money, I don't have access to the money. But what if I give you half my knowledge? And in return, what if you give me some of yours? In these kinds of knowledge exchanges, both parties walk away wealthier. Millennials understand this knowledge exchange better than anyone.

Millennials see money as just one piece of the wealth equation. Other pieces include knowledge, skills, and abilities, because if they don't possess these things, they consider themselves poor. Millennials are much more eager to work with other bright, creative, and talented people and share their knowledge because they understand that sharing builds wealth.

Millennials do, however, pose specific problems for recruiters. They thrive on teamwork and networking, have a low respect for authority, and have grown up with distinctly different social norms than earlier generations. Millennials see flip-flops as shoes and nose rings as perfectly acceptable business attire. More important, they are tech-savvy and prefer to do much of their research and information gathering online. If you and your company don't have a compelling online presence, recruiting Millennials can be a problem. An elementary Web site is a must. A site with all the whistles and bells is better. The premier solution is to create an online career center—a job application portal with job postings, company background, application forms that are easy to complete, and a real-time connection to your enterprise system.

In 2004, TargetX, a leading provider of interactive marketing technology and services to nearly four hundred and fifty colleges and universities, launched a division called iRecruit that challenged the college admissions world with a new approach to recruit Millennials. iRecruit is designed to give universities and businesses a cost-effective way to handle the recruiting process online and offers customized application forms, a campus visit scheduler, applicant tracking, and reporting. iRecruit's Internet student-recruiting applications helped attract Millennials to prestigious universities across the nation including, Columbia, the University of Miami, Drexel University, and others, and was responsible for a 42 percent increase in company revenue in 2004.

Here are a couple of ideas for recruiting Millennials:

Mention the Internet in your recruitment strategy. Create media that is upbeat; focus on unique ways to deliver information, including links to recruiter and future coworkers that might serve as company references; and provide videos and video creation tools, and access to company sites like Facebook, MySpace, YouTube, SecondLife, and CareerTV. Also, provide lots of online tools to help candidates learn about the company and interact with recruiters. Especially inventive companies are using instant messaging, blogs, blog ad networks, and job ads with comment capabilities to connect with candidates. Millennials are used to being marketed to and need a very distinctive message to get their attention. Some companies include testimonials from employees from different departments. A straightforward approach usually works best.

Your message doesn't have to be boring. At Google Inc., the leading Internet search engine on the planet, for example, the recruiting message is this: working at Google is fun, educational, and rewarding.

In just a few years, Google has developed a recruiting message that rings true for job candidates. At the same time, the company has promoted a genuine recruiting culture throughout the company. What that means is that recruiting permeates the organization from key leaders on down to the Gmail operations supervisor. Google funds its recruiting efforts with piles of money, but it also uses some interesting approaches to attract and retain employees. The most unique approach is to make the work itself the primary attraction. Working at Google is fun, educational, and rewarding because Google's leadership team ensures that all employees are working on interesting projects, learning continuously, constantly being challenged, and feel they're adding value.

At Google, selling just about any professional-level job is made easier because of senior management's commitment to what it calls "20-percent time," a policy that allows employees to work the equivalent of one-day-a-week on their own projects the company funds and supports. Other tech firms, like Genentech and 3M, have similar programs to attract and retain employees. Creative recruiting and incentive plans are about finding ways to excite employees. It's easy to understand why "20-percent time" excites computer programmers, engineers, and product managers. Google is about technical innovation. What is your company about?

What is your company especially good at? What exactly about your company makes an employee proud to work for you? How do you and the senior management team sell yourself to potential clients, business partners, shareholders, and most importantly your employees? These same benefits, whatever they are, need to be communicated to potential employees in a way that allows them to imagine themselves a part of your team.

Remember the days when you could just go to a few college fairs, put out some brochures, and wait to be contacted? Not anymore.

Today, recruiting professionals, not job candidates, do the door-banging. To attract Millennials fresh out of the colleges, you must begin knocking on doors early. Target not only the current graduates, but underclassmen. Talk to them about your company and why it's a great place to work. Do internship programs with freshmen and sophomores. Even go to high schools and get the kids excited about your products and services.

Make sure your focus is addressing the question, "What's in it for me?" (WIIFM). Your marketing materials should be high-tech and snazzy. They should speak the language of the Millennials. Send your marketing points by text message. Encourage potential employees to subscribe to your blog. (Make sure you have a blog.) Contribute to forums like industry blogs or podcasts. Send your youngest recruiters to show up at college job fairs and high school career days. Yes, it takes a while for a high-school junior to finish high school, college, and maybe an advanced degree in engineering, environmental science, or architecture. But if your organization is the first to implant the idea that your organization is the place to work, it's likely the student will give you first shot in the recruiting process.

Millennials are accustomed to having their voices heard and taken seriously and are readily willing to express their opinions. They may express their desire to meet with the CEO or be promoted early on in their employment. As a group, these young people are brash. They may be easily bored and may have short attention spans. The flipside is that Millennials deeply respect their elders and their opinions. The Millennial generation looks to their parents for advice and direction, and they count on their elders to be ardent supporters. It's not uncommon for Millennials entering college or looking for a job to ask the college or company if their parents can accompany them on an interview, so they can listen and advise. This degree of respect for age and experience is an advantage when building mentoring programs or transferring institutional knowledge from tenured employees to new recruits.

There is no question that the Millennial attitude can come off as arrogant. In terms of work style, Millennials expect to have the best technology, the best tools, and the best work environment. They often choose an organization based solely on who best automates the work process. But make no mistake, if given the right tools and the right work environment, this generation is committed to contributing and making their mark on the world.

Latching onto Xers, Boomers, and Traditionalists

What about recruiting Xers, that scarcer population who will be running things a few years from now? Xers tend to rely on advertisements and search firms to locate their next job. While Xers are tech-savvy, few use the Internet to search for a job. What this means is that recruiting campaigns that worked for Millennials don't work for Xers.

Recruiting campaigns come in many flavors, but Xers like to keep things simple. Begin by asking current Xer employees for recommendations. Encourage employees to recruit friends and family members, and you might offer a cash reward of some sort or a formal Employee Referral Program. Organizations are offering everything from iPods to laptops for employees who recommend new hires who stick it out for ninety days or more. Consider recruiting students from work-study programs. Get proactive in the community and become a member of the advisory committee that supports your local vocational programs.

When you talk with Xers, it's critical to earn their respect and know they will take a while to demonstrate that respect for you. Know that fun is serious business. Interject a little humor into your standard recruiting message or interview process. Anything, including silly practical jokes, will help to create a stimulating and productive recruiting environment. Interviews can be a chore, but whatever you do, don't look bored or glance over their shoulders. Don't give the impression that the interview isn't important or that it's just one more hurdle in the long grind of earning a job at your company.

Once you bring on a new candidate, try a reverse mentoring program where younger, newer workers are mentoring older workers about technology, science, social networks, consumer culture, gaming, or any other subject that a younger worker may understand and be willing to share. And last, let Xers know how they are doing as soon as possible. For example, give surprise rewards for unusual achievements.

Now let's talk Boomers.

Boomers don't plan to hang up their work clothes. They may retire, but it's equally likely they will continue to work in some manner. Their reasons for continuing to work include financial support, learning new skills, pursuing a dream never explored, building a social network, staying active and young at heart, or fulfilling the opportunity to give back to their community.

A friend of mine, who at fifty fulfilled her long-held dream of becoming a freelance writer, says, "I knew if I didn't change my life now, I would regret it later when it would be too late." Another fifty-plus acquaintance says, "I'm tired of being a slave, of getting into my suit and driving twenty miles to work every day. I just want to do what makes me happy, and now is the time to do it, because if I don't, it's not going to happen."

Many Boomers have enough money in the bank to spend some of that dough on long-held dreams, and often those dreams involve working for themselves. Their children may be grown and their expenses under control. If it wasn't for the cost of rising health care, Boomers would transition to free agency faster than they are. Some will continue to work full time, and many will work part-time by reducing their hours or responsibilities. Others will take jobs completely unlike those they held for the majority of their pre-retirement years. Ironically, many will be interested in jobs for which, in conventional terms, they are "over-qualified" and possibly not considered. Taken as a whole, Boomers will continue to work. They'll fit work into life, travel, grandkids, and hobbies. Therefore by definition, this group of semi-retiring Boomers will join the ranks of free agency. Having the opportunity to work with more flexible hours, levels of authority, and skills meets the needs of many Boomers. In knowledge capital alone, the Boomers' continued presence in the workforce is somewhat of a "life preserver" for many companies, especially those without a formal organizational learning program to transition a company's knowledge from one generation to the next.

Boomers and Traditionalists alike have their own approach to finding jobs. They network. These two generations have decades worth of Rolodex cards piled high with names and phone numbers of colleagues and coworkers. To attract Boomer and Traditionalist candidates, you must tap into your own networks as well as those of your employees.

Boomers are more and more likely to change their career paths in order to land positions in middle or upper management, which are more limited than entry-level posts. To attract Boomers, create a recruiting campaign with ample career transition support—career counseling, mentoring programs, career support groups, and workshops with guest speakers. Boomers want to see materials that illustrate an age-diverse workforce and may want more feedback and personal interaction during the interview process. Nonmonetary incentives such as continuous learning, autonomy, or time to pursue charitable interests may be as effective as money in attracting a talented older worker.

Chapter Four

Rewarding the Things
That Matter

"Different strokes for different folks."

—American idiom

Many Xers are angry at Corporate America. In the last dozen years or so, Xers have experienced a rash of layoffs, mergers, and restructurings. Many have relocated to find better jobs only to be transferred, laid off, merged, or restructured once again. The upshot is that Xers don't feel any loyalty to any company. This attitude puts recruiting executives in a tough spot and makes creating a reward and incentive program all the harder.

Millennials aren't much happier with Corporate America. Their biggest gripe is the smothering feeling of technology lockdown. College grads take what they believe is a good job, only to be issued crummy mobile phones and laptops. When they log onto the company's Intranet, they see a Web site that looks so 1990s it is laughable. The site doesn't have interactive features, such as Facebook, no ability to download iTunes, and no instant messaging. In many cases, they're hit with a security policy that forbids using personal e-mail like Hotmail. If this isn't the image of technology lockdown for a Millennial, then what is?

What does this have to do with creating a reward and incentive program? The answer is that if Xers want to take care of themselves under all circumstances (including layoffs and downsizing) by taking positions that allow them to gain fresh, marketable skills, build a strong network of contacts, and put money in the bank, then why not use these elements in your company incentive programs? If Millennials abhor rigid rules and worship digital freedom, then why not rethink your technology strategy to make it work in your favor?

Many companies still offer employee rewards and incentive plans based on tenure. However, in an economy of continuous off-shoring and downsizing, employee tenure can be elusive. Savvy employees, on the other hand, are looking for opportunities to learn and grow, rather than a lifelong career at one firm. To be competitive, employers should consider a variety of reward programs that meet the needs of a generationally diverse workforce. One possible approach is to maintain two separate incentive programs—a tenure-based incentive program for older employees, who prefer to stay with one employer indefinitely, and a more creative reward and incentive program aimed at addressing the changing needs of Millennials, Xers, and a handful of Boomers.

Traditional reward and incentive plans include annual bonuses, cash for meeting specific performance targets, profit sharing, and stock options. These plans have been around for years and are well documented in countless books and online sources. Incentive plans for a generationally diverse workplace, however, are not so well documented precisely because the plans are new, innovative, and sometimes counter to long-held command and control management strategies.

Worldwide consumer goods maker Unilever, for example, is trying to bridge the tech divide by allowing employees to use popular, often free, commercial software programs and products on company laptops. By moving users outside the company's firewall and allowing employees to connect to the Intranet via their own computers, Unilever sidesteps the issue of corporate security and gives users the digital freedom they want. In this way, employees simply load up their laptops with the software and applications they want. The list of free software is mind boggling—iTunes (music), LimeWire (file sharing), Camfrog Video Chat (real-time video streaming), PrimoPDF (document management), WorkTime (project management), QuickBooks Simple (accounting), Smart-Draw (flowcharts), Mindjet MindManager (process planning), and others. The idea isn't to turn employee laptops into a digital toy box, but to give employees the freedom to be more productive. For instance, Unilever encourages users to install inexpensive Webcams so they can videoconference instead of wasting time in airports and on freeways.

What makes a good employee incentive? That all depends on the employee. Boomers want an exit strategy that includes a pocket full of cash, pension options, and health care coverage. Xers want multiple career paths, annual increases, tuition reimbursement, flexible schedules, weekend getaways, and professional development. They also want flextime, leadership training, recognition, and the option to work from home when the opportunity is available. Millennials want technology, including iPods, computers, televisions, and digital freedom. They also want pay and management development, but they are equally motivated by tickets to sports and cultural events and gift certificates to Amazon and Netflix, and upscale designer stores like Victoria's Secret, Scoop NYC, J Brand, Louis Vuitton, Dell, Bose, and La Perla.

The first step in creating a reward program for individual generations is to stop thinking of your incentive plan as a one-way transaction. Too often, companies see rewards as nothing more than a costly expense rather than a long-term investment. In the good old days, a company car was the pinnacle of company perks. Today it's typically technology in the form of laptops with DVD, CD-ROM, and more gigabytes than the FBI's mainframe.

The hottest perks on the rewards scene are laptops, phones with PDA capabilities, and connectivity tools that make employees feel they are indispensable. The leading Internet search engine Google Inc., for example, is way ahead of the curve in providing innovative employee incentives. Google gives subsidized broadband to employees, free or subsidized mobile phones, free T-shirts, free all-you-can-eat meals in the cafeteria, and if that's not enough, the company runs a bus service in the San Francisco Bay Area to pick up and drop off employees. There's more. The company offers on-site health care, dental care, laundry service, and a gym.

And before you throw up your hands and list all the reasons you can't compete with Google, let me tell you don't have to. All you have to do is create an incentive plan that attracts the best talent in your industry. If you're in the Internet search engine industry, then you've got your work cut out for you. But most of us work in other industries where we've got a shot at becoming the gold standard for employee perks.

One company I recently worked with provided long-term executive leadership training to key staff. This was a good benefit in itself, but what made it exceptional was that the training team gave away Apple iPods to every employee who attended the training. Each iPod was preloaded with leadership training podcasts that allowed attendees to listen to lectures and interviews at their convenience, at home, while working out, or on the road. Given the popularity of iPods, it was a brilliant idea. So who thought of it? The CEO gave credit to one of his youngest staff members, a Millennial, wouldn't you know. But it wasn't just youthful Millennials and Xers who loved the idea. Boomers and Traditionalists went gaga over the gadgets.

Consider offering career development accounts—an allotment of training dollars per employee, per year, that permits each employee to create an individual training program. Employees can use the money to take online classes, enroll in university programs, and attend industry conferences, seminars, and events. Classroom training is great for some and a turn-off for others. Boomers love the camaraderie of college courses. Xers flock to online courses. Millennials crave interaction—multimedia, simulations, virtual settings, and communal learning. Every generation wants choice. The flexibility of career-development accounts meets the needs of your age-diverse workforce.

Another somewhat outside-the-box idea is turning your cafeteria into a company perk. Why not make the food free? At an average cost of $10 per day in food charges per employee, the cost to the company might run $2,500 per year per employee to offer three meals a day. Instead of increasing starting salaries, why not try free food. The key to making this program a genuine incentive is to play it up, announce the free food, and make a show of the program. This is one perk that applies equally to big shots and support staff and gives the impression of an organization that cares about everyone including its hourly workforce. The free food program can even include free sodas, sports drinks, snacks like trail mixes, and of course breakfast, lunch, and dinner. A side benefit of free breakfasts is that it might get workers to the office a little earlier and offer a healthier alternative and save on benefits.

A somewhat intangible perk that appeals to almost everyone is the trend of setting up anonymous company bulletin boards for workers to congregate and discuss workplace issues. These issues can range from common gripes about the boss to the lack of Ding Dongs in the vending machines to feedback about the company's latest products and marketing strategies.

What about day care? Google offers day care. Why can't your organization? Google opened its day care center, Kinderplex, in 2005, and more recently launched a second center, called the Woods, which follows the Reggio Emilia teaching philosophy, a learning approach that caters to each individual child. The service was never free, but Google subsidized the program to make it more affordable. Part of the subsidy offered kids a free breakfast, lunch, and snacks.

Rewarding Employees Strategically

A successful rewards and incentive program is about more than finding the next big thing to attract employees. It's about creating a total rewards program that can make a difference in how your company successfully grows your employee talent pool and your business. It's about rewarding the things that matter. And before you can do that, you have to understand what motivates key segments of your workforce.

One after another, companies have found rewards and perks are a powerful motivational tool and, when used strategically, can boost bottom-line revenue. Flexible incentives are a strategic tool that can help align business activities with business objectives.

A flexible rewards program is a system of benefits and incentives that typically consists of a combination of compensation, benefits, incentive plans, and perks (laptops and the like) that employees receive in exchange for their performance. In short, a flexible rewards system may impact the way employees identify and perceive their individual value to the company. In other words, load up new recruits with the latest technology, and employees feel valued. Or, toss out Mauritius-made golf shirts with the company logo during orientation, and new employees are likely to feel anything but special. This initial perception will have a direct effect on the employee's willingness to perform. Your rewards program is a crucial part of your talent retention strategy, and it's critical that you regularly review all components of your rewards systems in order to ensure you still maintain a competitive edge.

Although most employee reward plans include the basics, many organizations underestimate the value of strengthening nonmonetary rewards like work-life balance. Creation of a unique work-life program may set you apart from your competition and help to attract and retain key talent.

Work-Life Balance

Ask around. How many people do you know who don't think their job is stressful? One solution is to quit your job. Another is to find a job you enjoy and that leaves you enough time outside of work to have a life. At the core of work-life balance are two simple concepts: achievement and enjoyment. These answer the question of why we work. Achievement addresses personal development, career, and income. Enjoyment addresses the issues of joy, happiness, and meaning.

How you insert a positive work-life balance program into your organization is no easy task, but I would suggest you begin with enjoyment first. Specifically, it's helpful to begin with meaning. I'm referring to what really matters. Another way to think about work-life balance programs is to ask your employees what matters to them. The response will likely be a combination of children, spouse, career, money, spirituality, adventure, travel, health, sports, and technology. Remember we are trying to reward and incentivize employees by making work-life balance a strategic benefit in order to drive higher performance and boost overall employee retention. There are things you can do to improve the work-life balance for your employees.

First, try dropping all unnecessary activities. Scratch the marginally helpful meetings. Drop extremely tight deadlines when they aren't crucial. Second, protect your employee's private time. If it's the weekend and the staffer isn't scheduled to work, then don't intrude. Hold off on that call, e-mail, or text message until Monday morning. Get in the habit of scheduling your e-mail and text messaging to key employees to arrive during work hours. Third, partner with executive coaching and counseling professionals to give employees an objective voice to help with career and personal decisions. Fourth, plan enjoyable, fun, and adventurous activities. How about yoga classes, skiing trips, shared vacations to the rain forest in India or Door County, Wisconsin?

Outdoor clothing maker REI, for example, offers employees a 30 percent discount on trips scheduled through its own travel company, REI Adventures. REI made the 2007 list of Fortune's 100 Best Companies to Work For. The outdoor gear maker ranked number twenty-seven overall and number one in work-life balance. Other work-life balance perks include a $3,000 discount on adoption costs for parents eligible for the REI Flex Plan, a customizable health benefits program, and a four-week sabbatical for long-tenure employees. REI isn't the only company offering sabbaticals; Adobe Systems, American Express, Nike, Container Store, and Men's Wearhouse are doing the same.

Scheduling Wisely

A survey carried out by Merrill Lynch entitled "The New Retirement Study," found that nearly three-quarters of US Boomers plan to continue to work during retirement. There are lots of reasons for extending their careers: money, a change in career or industry, passing on knowledge, ongoing personal development, and we are living longer. The simple truth is that working retirees are often happier than those who retire and don't work. An added benefit is that working retirees are less likely to fear the spiraling costs of health care and future debt. When asked about the perfect work setup during retirement, Boomers and Traditionalists unanimously said finding the right combination of work and leisure.

The bottom line is that older Americans want to work and will work. The question is, does your organization have programs and policies that encourage older workers to choose your company over your competition?

Ongoing career development is about helping individuals manage their careers within and between organizations. It may seem counterintuitive, but offering creative work schedules is one way to help employees manage their careers. In a workforce study by the Florida recruitment agency Spherion in 2004, nearly three of four workers said they are willing to put their careers on the back burner to make time for family. All this sounds like employees would rather be at home than at work, but that's not the case. Flexible work schedules boost productivity. At the same time, flexible schedules can perk up your employee retention stats. For Boomers, a creative work schedule means finding alternatives to the traditional nine-to-five workday. In fact, if it works for Boomers, why not for Xers and Millennials?

One option is good old flextime, where employees work core hours but otherwise get to come and go as they please. Some employees might want to take a Web design class or watch a daughter's soccer games. Others will duck out to attend an economics course at the local university. Those with a long commute might want to come in at 6:30 a.m. so they can be home in time to spend the evening with family. Another popular flex-time option is switching to a four-day, ten-hour work week.

Part-time work is always an option. Consulting firm Business Talent Group allows consultants a combination of full- and part-time work. Depending on the project, consultants may work several full-time weeks and then take several weeks off. Consultants can also elect to share a project with another partner and each work half-time or some combination of hours that keep the client and their employer happy. Similar to the Business Talent Group approach, pillow manufacturer Boppy Company offers sales and other professional staff an option to split a full-time position. The difference is that the Boppy Company option is a permanent arrangement where each worker works twenty-four hours per week on different days with one day overlap.

Most of these options are not generationally driven but apply to different generations in different ways. Boomers may want to take you up on the offer to split a full-time job. Xers may want flexibility for its own sake. Remember that Xers have a nontraditional approach to time. Their attitude is: "As long as I get my work done, what does it matter when I'm in the office?" This isn't arrogance. It's just a different way of looking at the value they bring to your company. In their mind, that value has nothing to do with sitting at a desk from nine to five. Their value is in what and how they contribute.

Whatever your approach to rewards and incentives, keep repeating this mantra: "Options and flexibility . . . options and flexibility . . ."

One of my international clients made a hiring mistake by ignoring the law of flexibility. They wanted to fill a key executive position and finally found the perfect candidate, a woman with twenty-three years of experience and a resume to die for. They offered her a suitable salary and some key perks. One of these perks was the company's standard two-week vacation for the first five years of employment. In her last executive position, she received six weeks of vacation per year. The job candidate had worked hard for her vacation pay, and she wasn't willing to give it up. My client, on the other hand, stuck to the policy and thought nothing of asking this senior-level executive to start all over with two weeks of vacation a year. Why? Because it was policy. Needless to say, the candidate didn't take the job. The lesson here is that policy must bow to flexibility. You must be sensitive to the needs and wants of your employees and how these needs affect career decision-making.

Retiring in Style

With all this talk of youngish Xers and Millennials just entering the workplace, what about retirement services and programs as a reward-and-incentive-program element? Retirement options and financial planning services are a priority for all age groups and especially so for aging Boomers. There's no question that your recruiting management team must consider retirement benefits as a key component of your flexible incentive plan. Companies offering a wide variety of retirement and savings plans stand a better chance of meeting the financial needs of all employees. Plans might include voluntary retirement plans, tax deferred plans, short-term or long-term disability plans.

The downside to traditional retirement plans—money purchase pension plans, cash balance plans, profit sharing, 401(k) deferred tax plans, and employee stock ownership plan—is that many companies still require employees to work five or more years before becoming fully vested in the plan. This approach worked wonders for Traditionalists who valued tenure and Boomers who stuck around long enough to climb the corporate ladder. But Millennials and Xers aren't likely to take advantage of, nor be enamored with, programs with long-range vesting requirements. Therefore, these plans don't work as an incentive for recruiting and retention purposes. Far from it. Such plans reek of old-school thinking and can actually compel potential employees to choose another employer.

Retirement plans aside, whatever you do, don't offer just your traditional benefits. Think big. Get your management team to stretch in terms of offering incentives that people really care about. Drug maker AstraZeneca gives away company-made prescription drugs to all employees. Methodist Hospital System gives employees a $250 gas card each year, and WinStar Casino gives each employee a gas allowance with each paycheck, depending on how far they drive during each pay period. Quicken Loans offers workers in Michigan a ride on the company bus to Cleveland Cavalier basketball games. Law office Arnold & Porter pays employee referral fees of $15,000 for applicants who take the job. And software king Microsoft matches employee charitable contributions dollar-for-dollar up to $12,000. Each of these companies offers unique and unusual perks that help to retain employees and at the same time reinforce some aspect of the company mission.

It's your responsibility as an employer to know what your employees want. Once you've found the need, fill it. If you have employees who can't afford medical insurance, go out and buy a small, mini-med policy. Others want pet insurance—offer it. A segment of your workforce may want prepaid legal services where employees get access to legal counsel and advice from a qualified lawyer. You don't have to subsidize it, but why not offer it?

Highly Compensated Employees

Many employers are moving away from perks that help only highly compensated employees (HCE) because some employees perceive the programs as elitist, and the benefits may be considered discriminatory under the federal tax code. There may be good reasons to update your HCE perks to retain quality senior-level management.

Salary-based pension plans for HCEs contain contribution limits that often do not allow these highly compensated employees to save a proportionate percentage of their pay for retirement. To level the playing field, an employer can implement a non-qualified plan to provide incentives above the pension plan contribution limits. Non-qualified benefit plans are executive benefit programs whose primary purpose is to provide supplemental benefits to a company's key executives. These plans allow HCEs to defer taxable wages and bonuses until some future year when they're in a lower tax bracket. One creative non-qualified plan perk is to implement a payroll deduction program for health insurance, certain types of other insurance, and even the purchase of computer equipment.

Whatever your reward and incentive program, it's critical that it include benefits that motivate your entire workforce. Every generation is motivated by money, but Xers, for instance, want to work for a company that will enable them to gain marketable skills and prepare them for future projects and jobs. Millennials are motivated by laptops, Wii stations, iPods, and the latest cell phones. Whether your incentive program is heavy on tangibles like technology, cash, travel, and gift cards or focuses on intangibles like fun, recognition, career development, a free-spirited workplace, and positive reinforcement, the key is to reward workers in ways that encourage them to support the company's overall direction and strategy. Company rewards and incentives are simply one more tool to help organizations like yours turn multigenerational differences into a competitive advantage.

Chapter Five

Managing People, a Balancing Act

"I go to work and look at some of the young kids in our office. We're in a conservative financial planning firm but we have an employee with tattoos on her feet and one on her back. I'm shocked that no one asks her to wear shirt collars or Band-Aids to cover them."

—Traditionalist office worker

Managing workers in a multigenerational workplace can be a hotbed of conflict. Each generation has distinct attitudes, expectations, and habits with regard to work and career. Traditionalists, for example, are top-down managers. Boomers are optimistic and competitive. Xers are mistrustful of any management system. And Millennials are big on making a difference, and they want to do it in their way. Throw these four generations into a single workforce, and you've got the ingredients for disagreement.

In addition, workplace hierarchies are changing, and youngish Xers are now supervising older generations, both Boomers and Traditionalists. How then do you manage a diverse group of workers with distinct backgrounds, world views, and objectives? The short answer is: strive to be flexible with sensitivity.

Directing Traditionalists

Several generations in the workplace means differing views about loyalty, work ethic, respect, freedom, and rewards. The oldest worker cohort, Traditionalists, are now in their sixties, seventies, and early eighties. Loyal to a fault, Traditionalists expected and continue to expect to build a lifetime career with one employer, or at least in a single field, and to make a lasting contribution. This is all well and good, but if Traditionalists are all but retired, what's the big deal? The big deal is the growing trend toward delaying retirement, thus resulting in millions of Traditionalists remaining at work. Even though the youngest Traditionalists are in their late sixties, until they retire, they remain a viable segment of the workforce.

Managing Traditionalists amidst the changing workplace demographics begins with understanding their core values. Tradition-alists' values are influenced by hardships—the Great Depression of the 1930s, the establishment of the Social Security System, the United States' preparation for World War II, the surprise attack on Pearl Harbor by the Japanese navy, the D-Day Invasion of Normandy by Western Allied forces in an effort to liberate Europe from Nazi occupation during World War II, and America's involvement in the Korean War. The children of the 1920s and 1930s grew up with a weight on their shoulders. More importantly, they have survived many hardships with a deep faith and consequently view themselves as survivors.

Traditionalists value privacy, trust, and hard work. They believe in paying their dues and are irritated when others don't do the same. Their word is their bond. They respect authority and social order. Their career is who they are. Traditionalists are conformists and history-oriented. They make decisions based on what worked or didn't work in the past. They like details and are uncomfortable with ambiguity. And last, they need to feel that their experience is appreciated.

Strategies to get the most from your Traditionalist workforce might include setting clear ground rules explaining your credentials, especially if you are an Xer or Boomer manager remembering that every generation has a story to tell and looking for common ground.

On being a young boss, and let's face it, most managers are younger than the typical seventy-something Traditionalist, you might try the following: respect experience and demonstrate this respect in the way you communicate with Traditionalists and in the projects you assign them. Don't worry about being talked down to. It's going to happen, and it has nothing to do with you personally. Go out and learn and make learning a habit. Learning involves study but it also involves being humble, a trait Traditionalists will adore. Constant learning also involves admitting that you don't know it all and asking others for advice and information. When outlining duties and roles to your Traditionalist workforce, don't assume the Traditionalist's way is your way. In other words, once you lay out the goal, don't assume the approach of a Traditionalist will be anywhere close to the approach you would have taken. It may not be, and it doesn't have to be.

Whatever you do, involve Traditionalists in the plan, be it a process change, new marketing strategy, or a routine work schedule adjustment. Keep them informed. Let them know why decisions were made, how the plan will unfold, and their role in the process. When all else fails, connect with and manage Traditionalists by doing what Traditionalists do: be loyal, have patience, be a team player, and make your boss and your subordinates look good. Traditionalists are slow to come around to change, however they are usually the best sales people in any organization; be patient and take the time necessary to train them on the technology and you will be surprised at the amazing results. Remember they can mentor your Millennials and Xers.

Governing Boomers

Boomers are egocentric. As a manager, sharing information with fellow Boomers can be difficult. Peer competition and egos often get in the way of progress, and to make matters worse, Boomers demand constant change. They are hard to please and ever ready to move on to a new position. Remember, Boomers started the workaholic trend. Their work is their life, and they are still committed to climbing the ladder of success.

The upside to managing Boomers is that they were one of the first generations to meet the challenge of communicating across generations. Boomers were the first to understand and use generational language. They know the lingo, and this lingo does not always involve words. Communicating to a Boomer or Traditionalist might mean formal writing and speaking. To techno-savvy Xers and Millennials, communicating often means e-mail and instant-messaging. Being aware of generational differences like language can help you anticipate miscommunications and tailor your message for maximum effect.

Communicating with Boomers can be tricky. Boomers are the "show me" generation, and it's important to use body language to reinforce ideas that might not ring true using words alone. They favor a personable style of communication that aims to build rapport. Be open. Learn the importance of structuring emotionally meaningful, relevant, and positive messages. Speak clearly and directly. Use face-to-face talks when possible and follow it up with e-mail to ask for feedback. Encourage and answer questions in a way that addresses all the concerns, even those not specifically asked. Know in advance that Boomers will press you for details and it's critical that you have those details handy in the form of notes, handouts, PowerPoint presentations, or any other format that shows you have thoroughly thought through your message or plan. Whatever you do, avoid controlling language that may come off as manipulative or one-sided, and present alternatives to show flexibility in your thinking.

To manage your Boomer workforce better, discover why Boomers behave the way they do. In most cases, this means understanding that Boomers are people who work to live. Boomers are competitive and willing to make sacrifices for success. At the same time, they stubbornly maintain their hold on remaining forever young and in turn have influenced the expectations of the generations that follow. They believe in and support the executive branch of the government and at the same time mistrust major American corporations. In the 1960s and early 1970s, Boomers protested against war and shouted for a smaller military. Today, in response to the global war on terrorism, Boomers are supportive of the military. Like the Traditionalists, Boomers favor a top-down approach and value respect and recognition. They have also reshaped corporate culture with casual dress and flexible schedules.

Organizational development scholar, Dr. Morris Massey, argues that our behaviors are driven by our value system or our value programming. Boomers' values are closely rooted to the value system in vogue when Boomers were in their twenties and thirties.

By examining this value system, you can better understand Boomer beliefs and behaviors. I'm not suggesting that you have to agree with these values, but you can strive to understand the mind-sets of each generational group.

A part of the Boomer value programming is what they didn't experience. Boomers didn't suffer economically hard times as their parents did. On the contrary, they had the good life. The difference between Traditionalists and Boomers is that Boomers value hard work because they view it as necessary for moving to the next level of success while Traditionalists work hard because they feel it's the right thing to do. Boomers value success and teamwork and inclusion, which partially explains the Boomer penchant for frequent meetings to keep everyone informed and give everyone on the team a voice in the decision-making. And last, Boomers don't appreciate rules for the sake of having rules.

Supervising Xers

Xers range in ages from twenty-seven to forty-seven. This group is fed up with corporate antics. This I've-had-enough attitude has led many Xers to start their own businesses. A large percentage of Xers didn't attend college. Others attended schools one after another. Unlike Boomers, Xers don't climb ladders. They move from job to job or position to position in order to broaden their skills. They are sponges for technical knowledge. It's important to communicate and manage in ways that make sense to this youngish generation.

Ignoring a significant age difference between you and your younger (or older) employees may work for a little while, but eventually you'll need to address this growing, though tricky, workplace issue. Here are several ways for successfully managing your Xer employees. They want self-development through independent learning. Make self-development an overt part of the job. They prefer specific jobs with concrete goals. Unlike Traditionalists, and to some degree Boomers, Xers have an unyielding interest in balancing work life and personal life. Xers crave constant stimulus. They love fun. They hate routine and are consequently viewed as unmotivated, outspoken, self-centered, and job-hoppers. As much as Boomers hate rules, it's Xer managers and specialists who are more likely to go around rules and take chances.

If Xers have a common communication credo, it would be this: they believe in mutual respect, open communications, and the willingness to listen. It sounds a lot like Boomers with one exception: Xers can respectfully disagree and move forward with a project or strategy. Xers don't assume they know the intentions behind each other's words. When confused, they ask. Xers avoid blame and, therefore, don't expect to be blamed when things go wrong. While Xers prefer texting and e-mail, when they have a disagreement with another team member, they're not opposed to having a face-to-face to clear the air. Xers love to focus on issues, situations, and tasks—not on people.

When it comes to work ethic, it's important that you trust your Xer workers. Give them options. Let Xers with families telecommute or work outside business hours when necessary and know that this little bit of flexibility will work wonders to build loyalty. Telecommuting may even save you some money. In a 2008 poll of fifteen hundred technology workers conducted by Dice Holdings Inc., 37 percent said they would accept a salary cut if allowed to work from home. Eighty-four of the Fortune 100 Best Companies to Work for 2008 allow employees to telecommute or work at home at least 20 percent of the time. Networking equipment-maker Cisco Systems has 70 percent of its workforce telecommuting. Financial giant Principal Financial Group, ranked number twenty-one on Fortune's list, has 23 percent of its workforce working from home. Telecommuting or not, you will score points with Xer employees by keeping the office environment up-to-date. How about offering music at work, BlackBerrys, instant messaging, and super fast computers.

When negotiating with Xers, be flexible. Xers are marketable and they know it. Other Xer management tips include limiting in-person meetings and instead arranging conference calls and video and Web conferencing when needed. Limit bureaucracy. Provide access to information and resources without the drudgery of corporate politics. Xers are casual by nature. Give them a heads-up if they should dress for meetings. Treat them as partners rather than underlings. They thrive on change and are used to being challenged, so challenge them with big projects.

Managing Millennials

Millennials are sociable, optimistic, talented, and a hot commodity on the job market. What makes managing Millennials somewhat unique is that they are arriving in the workplace with higher expectations and very little workforce experience than previous generations. If an employer doesn't match those expectations, they are likely to spread the word.

Growing up, Millennials were bombarded with consistent and compelling messages. Parenting patterns molded a new generational perspective, an era with its own mood and influences. These messages included things like: be smart, be inclusive and tolerant, stay connected 24/7, decide what you want, go for it, and serve your community.

In 2006, Cone Inc., a Boston-based brand strategy firm, surveyed eighteen hundred thirteen- to twenty-five-year-olds and found that 79 percent want to work for a company that cares about its impact on society. Sixty-four percent said their employer's social activities, including volunteering, inspired loyalty. A first-rate corporate volunteer program can, in fact, help you manage your Millennial workforce. Banking giant PNC Financial Services Group created an employee volunteer program that includes partnerships with roughly two hundred nonprofits nationwide. Employees can choose between skills-based volunteer assignments (performing volunteer accounting for a small South American business) or projects unrelated to their jobs (working with local childhood education programs), and the company will pay the employees' salary for the time away from the office.

Target Corporation has partnered with VolunteerMatch, an online database that pairs volunteers and nonprofits. By logging in, Target employees can access a list of 55,300 nonprofits, choose a program that appeals to them, and sign up. General Electric Company offers a different volunteering approach. The company arranges for employee volunteers to tutor elementary school children from local Philadelphia public schools and does so within the GE offices. A GE program for high-schoolers teaches networking, interviewing, and resume-building skills. These types of volunteer programs are tied to efforts to retain two major employee groups, younger workers looking for work-life balance, and ready-to-retire older workers who want to serve their communities.

Barry Salzberg, chief executive officer of Deloitte LLP, says that Millennials demand choices. They want to be valued and noticed for their contribution. In a Town Hall Los Angeles speech in May 2008, Salzberg said, "What I find most exciting is that Millennials are changing how all the generations work together."

So how do you, as a manager, translate your younger workers' inherent wish for choices like volunteering into the day-to-day management on the job? Phrased differently, the question might be what kind of management processes work best with Millennials? Here are a few approaches that work:

Lead by example. Millennials have grown up with structure and supervision, with parents who were role models. Millennials are looking for leaders with honesty and integrity. Challenge them. Millennials want to learn. They want to try new things. They want growth and not just to master a single job skill or position. Let them work with people they like. Millennials strive to get in sync with friends and coworkers. Employers who enhance the social aspects of the job such as working with friends, group projects, collaborative learning, and online social networking tools will be well rewarded. It may sound counterproductive, but why not interview and hire friends as a group? Millennials want to have fun. Humor and silliness are okay as far as Millennials are concerned. They also want respect and for their ideas to be respected. Be flexible. Millennials won't give up activities they care about just because of a job, and an inflexible schedule is one of many ways to encourage your Millennial workforce to head for the doors.

Managing a multigenerational workforce is a balancing act. As a manager, you must learn to recognize and understand the expectations of each generation and create harmony, mutual respect, and genuine teams. It can be helpful in this process to examine your own generational patterns and identify opportunities for expanding your cross-generational communication skills. A good first step is to be self-aware. Know your own biases and recognize that others may not share those biases. Understand that conflicts among employees are often a result of conflicting values and less often about disputes over company policy or procedures.

When resolving generational conflicts, address the behaviors that impact performance and do so in a way that is sensitive to the generational characteristics involved. For instance, Boomers typically want to include people and, therefore, hold lots of meetings. Xers are no fans of meetings and, given half a chance, will skip out early or miss the meeting entirely. Boomers may see a skipped meeting as a lack of respect. Xers see it as a time-saver. When addressing the issue, concentrate on the underlying values and attitudes and not simply on creating new scheduling policies or punishments around company meetings.

The next step is to focus on accommodating different styles. Allow employees to identify their views. Encourage employees to introduce new ideas and be open to them. Be flexible. Get it through your head that Xers and Millennials aren't workaholics and never will be. Recognize that work-life balance is a core value and create management processes and programs that promote or at least allow time for the whole person—job, career, personal development, family, volunteering, health and exercise, and special interests.

"I think that flexible hours is a great idea, Liz!
I will need to run the 'yoga lounge in the
break room' by corporate, though."

Chapter Six

Motivating the
Next Generation

"If you make a job as comfortable as you can, people
tend to stay longer. They look forward to coming to work.
The energy is higher and productivity rises."

—Lin O'Neill
Futures Consulting

Prior to starting my consulting practice, I was the vice president of
Human Resources and Risk for a full service international staffing
company with more than two hundred branches. My office was in
Dallas, and one day I was called to our payroll processing division
on the sixth floor. The director of Payroll explained that she had a
problem with a new employee who had been with the company less
than ninety days and wasn't following policy. I invited the young

lady, who was in her mid-twenties, into the conference room and asked a female supervisor to join us. The employee, let's call her Susan, had a dozen facial piercings on her ears, lips, eyebrows, nose, cheek, and even her tongue—all of which violated company dress code.

The facial jewelry wasn't the problem.

Her supervisor said that several female coworkers had complained that Susan came to work without a bra. According to the coworkers, they felt uncomfortable around her, and the sight of Susan braless was distracting male coworkers. I could see for myself that Susan had on a delicate see-through top without anything underneath. When I asked Susan why she came to work without proper undergarments, she said she wasn't blessed, meaning, I believe, that she didn't have large breasts. She said she had never worn a bra and didn't feel the need to wear one now.

"Have you read the company handbook?" I asked.

"Sure," Susan said.

"And the dress code policy?"

"I read it. But since no one asked me to remove my jewelry," she said touching her nose stud, "I thought it was okay to come to work without a bra."

According to Susan's supervisor, Susan was a model employee and she didn't want to lose her for policy violations. The policy indicated we fire Susan or, at a minimum, issue a written warning, and if the piercings or the lack of undergarments continued, then fire her. But this didn't make any sense. Susan was a well-trained, motivated, and productive employee who didn't have any face-to-face contact with customers. Common sense said there was another way.

We finally arrived at a compromise. During work hours Susan had to wear a bra, blessed or not, and she could continue to wear her jewelry as long as she remained in her current role and had no direct, visible customer contact. Win-win.

This solution was an example of meeting the intent of the company policy while keeping employees like Susan and her manager as motivated as possible and performing at their best.

Motivating Strategies

No workplace is more productive or competitive than a company filled with motivated employees. What can you do to keep workers motivated? Lots of things. Try offering exceptional training. Tax firm PricewaterhouseCoopers, for example, sent all five thousand employees of the firm's consulting arm to Orlando for a week-long training session, where, among other goodies, they received free iPod shuffles.

Treat all employees with respect and be tolerant of ethnic and religious differences. Know when employees are overworked and do something about it. Set clear goals. Show an interest in each employee's work output. Offer unique rewards and make the rewards something the employees value. Oklahoma oil and gas powerhouse Chesapeake Energy Corporation, for instance, offers employees free scuba lessons—in Oklahoma, no less. Employees earn their scuba-diving certification at classes in Chesapeake's on-site Olympic-size pool. The company hires the instructor and picks up the tab for instructional materials.

Provide positive feedback and say thank you. One way to say thank you is with money and discounts. One of the nation's largest multifamily real estate corporations, Camden Property Trust, offers employees who live in one of the firm's one hundred and eighty apartment complexes in San Diego, Denver, and Houston a 20 percent discount on rent. Employees can also vacation in one of

Camden's fully furnished properties for $20 a night. Remember that people are motivated by different things. Use what motivates your employees, not what motivates you.

One approach is to stop looking for commonalities among the generations. Start looking for differences. What motivates one group won't motivate another, so look for and identify those different motivational trigger points. Employees don't have to look alike. They don't have to dress alike. It's okay for a sixty-year-old Boomer and a twenty-two-year-old Millennial fresh out of college to look and behave differently.

Millennials, for instance, want social opportunities well beyond the annual Christmas party. Office productivity improves when coworkers are friends outside the office, according to 57 percent of executives polled by Accountemps, a staffing firm. To encourage social opportunities, consider a company-sponsored book club that meets at lunch, car pooling, an international cuisine night where spouses and friends gather at a different restaurant every few months, or the old standby—company-sponsored softball, basketball, and tennis. Recognize Millennials' high level of required social interaction. Use experiential learning and team assignments whenever possible. Give them freedom with regard to how and where they work.

As morally driven as the Millennial generation is, your firm will benefit if you make the work meaningful. At nonprofit Benetech, the company's stated mission is to create new technology solutions that serve humanity and empower people to improve their lives. This type of mission statement focuses almost solely on meaning and less on products, services, and profits. What the company actually does is not easily pigeon-holed. Benetech has several ongoing projects—Bookshare.org, a Web site that provides digital books to visually impaired readers; management consulting for conservation projects; software to measure human rights violations;

innovative technologies to promote humanitarian land mine removal efforts; and reading and writing programs for adolescent and adult readers. All of these projects are aimed at improving people's lives. Benetech's focus on the wider world is precisely the type of company Millennials will flock to.

Getting to the Core of Things

The key to motivating your workforce is understanding what each generation cares about. What do they need to do their jobs better, more efficiently, more comfortably, and more joyfully? Perhaps your workers want a kid-friendly atmosphere that encourages families to visit mom or dad at work or perhaps they would like on-site child care. Business intelligence and software leader SAS Institute was an early adopter of on-site child care, opening its first day care center in 1981. It now has four centers caring for more than six hundred children at a cost to employees of a reasonable $350 a month.

What if the bulk of your workforce doesn't work in an office? Trucking firms are motivating drivers by offering creature comforts in their trucks—custom seats, satellite radio, and microwave ovens. Handy microwave ovens might not get your employees excited, but for long-distance truckers, having an in-truck oven can be a powerful employee incentive. And why not offer community service options to your truck driver workforce? Professional truck drivers are constantly on the road and consequently rarely in their own community, which can make volunteering a challenge. Drivers often have no one to talk to and no one to share interesting anecdotes and insights. The nonprofit organization Trucker Buddy International has found a solution.

Trucker Buddy offers drivers an eager audience by pairing truckers with classes of schoolchildren. Each week drivers share news about their travels with their class, and once a month, students write letters to their drivers. The upside is twofold—drivers get a chance to share their experiences with children in communities they care about, and students' skills in reading, writing, geography, and math are enhanced by the relationship.

Motivating Xers

Human resource consultant and President of Futures Consulting Lin O'Neill says, "The key to working with the generations is to endorse them all. At the same time, why not tout what each new generation brings to the party?" What Xers bring to the party is attitude.

Xers work to live rather than live to work. In other words, Xers value having a life—a whole life, not just the one inside the office. They believe in maintaining a healthy work-life balance and appreciate managers who can understand that. Work-life balance programs, flexible work schedules, mobile offices, advanced technology, social networking sites, and college tuition reimbursement programs can all be used to motivate Xers to higher job performance.

Companies like nonprofit researcher MITRE encourage workers to get out of the office and go to school. The company offers tuition reimbursement up to $20,000 and bonuses for advanced degrees, which 65 percent of all workers hold. Family-owned supermarket chain Nugget Markets takes another approach to work-life balance issues. In 2007, Nugget took the entire company white-water rafting. What tuition reimbursement and white-water rafting trips have in common is that both demonstrate that the company cares about its employees. Show employees that you care about them. How you go about it is up to you. When the homebuilding industry slowed, homebuilder David Weekley Homes canceled its annual reward trip and tripled severance pay for laid-off employees.

Job sharing and telecommuting is another benefit that allows Xers a chance to spend more time away from the office. Job sharing is a flexible work arrangement where the responsibilities of a full-time position are split between two people. Telecommuting, on the other hand, allows employees to work from home. Do your employees really need to be on site to do their jobs? What if, for example, you handed out laptops to your data entry staff? Could the same work and performance levels be maintained by staff working from home? Office space is often at a premium, especially in urban areas; so employees who don't take up valuable office space can save a company considerable money. At-home workers also provide community benefits such as reducing pollution and traffic congestion, all while making your workers happier. And happier employees are always more productive, highly motivated employees.

An alternative to full-scale job sharing is to rethink your organization's system of phased retirement for Traditionalists and Boomers so workers are able to work part-time or "part-years." The University of North Carolina started a program that allowed faculty fifty years and over to work half-time for half salary for up to three years while collecting partial pension benefits. The program was started in 1998 and now almost one-third of retiring faculty at UNC campuses takes advantage of the phased retirement program. The university found a way to keep its most experienced faculty by providing programs that workers valued.

While we are talking part-time workers, how about insurance benefits as a motivational tool? Shipping firm FedEx Corporation, for example, offers health insurance to retirees and part-timers.

There are other ways to motivate the troops that won't cost you a penny. How about encouraging your C-level management team (CEOs, CFOs, CIOs, and others) to spend scheduled time with factory workers, office staff, and other frontline workers? I recently spoke to a CEO of a large manufacturing company. Let's call him Charles. Charles mentioned that his human resources manager recommended he boost morale by having breakfast with employees once a month.

"Did you take his advice?" I asked.

"Twice. But I'm not sold on the idea because the employees didn't seem all that engaged."

"What did they say?"

"Well, they didn't say much."

"So you just sat there for thirty or forty minutes and ate your breakfast."

"Far from it," the CEO said. "I talked nonstop."

I spoke with the HR Manager, and he confirmed that employees weren't engaged because the CEO never shut up. They didn't speak up because they weren't given a chance. The CEO relied on an old model of communication. No doubt Traditionalists would have pulled up a chair and listened, but most of his employees are twenty- and thirty-somethings, Xers most of them, and they tuned him out. If the CEO had been coached in generational differences, he might have taken a different tack and asked more open-ended questions, listened, and shown an interest in the core issues affecting his workforce rather than the issues affecting senior management or the company in general. The employees felt they were being preached to.

Leaders spending time with the troops can work. Shared Technologies CEO Tony Parella visited all forty-one locations to talk with workers in 2007, and employees loved the visits. If you don't have the time or inclination to do breakfasts or office visits, why not invite interested employees to come to you? Web-hosting firm Rackspace Managed Hosting values transparency and invites workers to attend bimonthly Open Book meetings, where all financial issues are put on the table for anyone interested enough to look and listen.

Mentoring and Motivation

We have talked about mentoring programs before, but the topic bears repeating. By pairing older, more experienced workers with younger, tech-savvy employees, you motivate both groups to build connections that might not have existed otherwise. And don't get stuck in the traditional paradigm of older workers passing along wisdom to their juniors. There is a great deal of value in reverse mentoring—younger workers who may have specific expertise in helping older workers become more comfortable with new ideas.

Employees involved in mentoring programs strive for excellence because they want to show others they are worthy. Even the smallest mentoring program can help boost morale and motivate employees to higher performance Programs can be as simple as guiding new-hires around the office for the first thirty days or as comprehensive as regular one-on-one meetings, counseling, and specific training. Here are some simple guidelines that apply to any company mentoring program: Establish the rules up front. Let everyone know what is expected of the people involved, the limits, and how long the program will run. Choose the mentor pairs wisely. You want a mentor with an impressive background and experience, but also someone who has the time, attitude, and a willingness to share.

Microchip maker Intel began its mentoring program way back in 1997. The idea is to match mentors with employees who need specific skills. In this way, the company spreads best practices quickly throughout the organization. As a benchmark, Intel uses written contracts and clear deadlines to make sure its mentoring program gets results.

A tangent to the reverse mentoring program I mentioned earlier is the younger-boss–older-employee dynamic. This relationship is becoming more common as the number of over–fifty-five workers grows. Employee motivation isn't a top-down phenomenon. More and more, younger workers will play a key role in motivating older workers. If a Traditionalist resists using new computer software, for example, it probably isn't because he is trying to be difficult. Rather, he is more familiar with the non-computer way of getting things done. He enjoys stability and practicality and is content with the old way of doing things. It's your job, as a younger manager, to motivate him to change.

Keep in mind that not long ago these older workers were young trendsetting executives just like you. Mr. Williams, for example, now an aging retiree was once the VP of a major fund-raising organization. When he was the boss, he viewed older workers as dead weight. He had the perception that older employees were tired, not as productive, and simply couldn't handle the workload of their younger coworkers. But since coming out of retirement a few months ago, he found himself on the other side of the fence.

It's not that he wanted to be in charge again. Mr. Williams wanted to be active and challenged. In fact, he didn't want the responsibility of running a business. He was happy to leave that task to his new boss, an intelligent, cocky thirty-something. Not surprisingly, Mr. Williams and his new boss had challenges to overcome, chiefly because of generational work styles and work ethic. Older workers like Williams want face time with the boss. They often come to work early and work long hours and weekends. Xers see in-person meetings as a drain on productivity, and they care less about when and where the work gets done so long as it gets done.

Xer managers are used to following up with e-mail and text messages, sometimes thirty or more an hour. They are more likely to say, "Send me an e-mail" than "Let's meet and talk it over." Younger workers are more willing to figure things out for themselves, and they secretly expect older workers to do just that—figure it out on their own. Nevertheless, the way to motivate older employees is to show them you value their contribution by taking the time to answer questions and share you thoughts. And keep in mind, this process isn't a one-way street. There are times when an Xer manager will need to tap into an older coworkers' knowledge and skills.

Coaching and Team-Building for Better Performance

Executive coaching programs can be a powerful motivational tool. Many forward-looking companies have used coaching programs with great success. Traditional training can only go so far. Yet when you combine training and corporate coaching, employee productivity explodes. Corporate educator Jo Anna Couch says, "Consulting firms who engage coaches estimate that teamwork can be improved as much as 75 percent in an organization, while conflicts among personnel are reduced as much as 25 percent."

Many organizations integrate coaching into leadership development. As part of the program, firms incorporate "360-degree" assessments from managers, coworkers, and employees that give the participant a better understanding of their strengths and weaknesses as viewed by others. The results of these assessments often pinpoint areas where an employee can benefit from working with a coach. Coaching is not just for tackling new projects or honing new skills but can also play an invigorating or motivating role. The one-on-one contact inherent in the coaching process is itself a motivating experience. In addition, coaches can help employees develop new ways to attack old problems or help employees who have perceptual blind spots recognize their deficiencies and take appropriate corrective action.

Team-building programs are another way to motivate your workforce. High-functioning teams can meet the needs of all generations. The next time you form a team—task force, problem-solving team, product-design team, committee, work group, or quality circle—bring in enough people so that all the generations are represented. Team-building and other corporate events like treasure hunts, ropes courses, and dynamic problem-solving exercises can help develop and motivate your teams. A highly motivated workforce has several things in common. Employees work together, develop loyalty, and get a kick out of coming to work.

Financial services firm American Century Investments is committed to the team concept. Each of the company's investment portfolios—small cap, mid cap, large cap growth, international growth, global growth—are managed by specialized and highly skilled teams. Newcomers at American Century are given a big welcome. Teams put up deskside banners or buy new recruits lunch. The attitude at American Century is to celebrate company successes and do it in a way that brings people together. Each time American Century exceeds previous company milestones (growth targets, assets under management), managers throw huge parties with live music, lavish food and drink, and custom-created, gold-dust sprinkled American Century cookies. The company treats employees to outdoor celebrations with champagne toasts from executives and flyovers by airplanes trailing congratulatory messages. At the company's 40th anniversary, employees joined in for a 1950s-style ice cream social.

Executive coaching and team-building are just two more ways to motivate your multigenerational workforce. Applied in creative ways, these programs can increase quality, improve leadership, enhance customer satisfaction, and get your employees revved up and enthusiastic about coming to work.

". . . well Dan, when HR suggested 'relating
with the younger hires' during training,
I don't think this is what they had in mind."

Chapter Seven

Generational Training Time

"Too often it seems that strategy and talent
management are not connected."

—Dr. Don Hanratty, President
The Career Control Group

Investing in generational training and learning can be a significant component of your company's overall competitive strategy. Generational training is the process of teaching people a set of leadership skills that encourage the highest performance from each generation in your workforce. The basic philosophy of any generational training program is to respect differences and encourage managers and frontline employees to appreciate and use these differences to increase productivity.

It's critical that your generational training program include two separate elements: 1) management training that helps managers recognize generational issues and 2) frontline employee training tailored to meet the needs of the distinct generations within your organization.

Generational Training for Managers

The first element, generational training for your management team, must include all the elements described throughout this book—identifying your generational mix, recruiting, rewarding, managing, motivating, training, and recognizing generational influences including values, seminal events, cultural memorabilia, heroes, and style.

Commerce Bank, an independent banking firm, has created such a generational training program and put together a curriculum to help bank managers better understand Traditionalists, Boomers, Xers, and Millennials and their roles in the workplace. The program was rolled out to the entire organization of more than five thousand employees. Commerce is heavily invested in training and development, increasing its training budget by 39 percent over the last five years, spending almost $3 million per year. One key to the company's long-term success is its private banking initiative, where experienced bankers are trained in complex personal finance and investing strategies. These bankers work directly with affluent customers, and in the last five years, profits from Commerce's private banking business doubled to $19 million.

Architecture firm HOK addresses generational training by setting targets to include a larger number of younger workers in leadership development opportunities. Marsha Littell directs HOK's generational training program for more than three hundred managers. She says that the dynamics at HOK are changing—52 percent of the workforce is under forty, and 19 percent of its 2,500 employees are between twenty and thirty. Xers and Millennials now outnumber Boomers and Traditionalists, and as more Boomers reach retirement, the percent of younger employees in leadership positions increases. To get ahead of the curve, HOK made sure at least 10 percent of attendees at the company's recent leadership meeting were Millennials.

Littell trains managers to remember that Millennials have a high self-worth. Performance reviews are important to this generation, but don't be surprised if they give themselves higher marks than you do. Performance reviews are a good opportunity for managers to listen and understand your Millennial worker's point of view before you offer your assessment. Overall, Millennials love performance reviews, so make the reviews regular and more frequent than you might otherwise for Xers and Boomers.

Enterprise Rent-A-Car responds to this need of its younger workers for regular interaction by encouraging management trainees to have daily contact with managers and participate in weekly meetings to go over performance goals. The company is one of the largest recruiters of college graduates in the nation, and a large part of its sixty thousand worldwide employees are Millennials and young Xers.

Not only are banks, architecture firms, and car rental agencies changing the way they train managers and employees to address generational concerns, but law firms are doing much the same. According to "The Changing Face of the Legal Industry"—a white paper from Robert Half Legal, an industry staffing service—law offices are investing in leadership development initiatives and business management training for senior-level lawyers (Boomers and Traditionalists), while associate-level staff (Xers and Millennials) participate in mentoring programs. Mentoring programs are an effective way to build professional networks, something your Millennial workforce craves, and at the same time identify skill gaps.

Fifteen partners at the law firm Miller, Canfield, Paddock and Stone volunteered to mentor two or three associates each and act as writing coaches. Junior-level associates wrote memos, letters, and settlement agreements, and the partners reviewed the work and gave concrete suggestions to make their thoughts and writing clearer. This program allowed associates to get some extra face time with a partner and allowed partners to gauge how well associates understood the business of law.

Miller Canfield's mentoring and training program isn't just about better writing. The firm recognizes that young lawyers grew up in a culture of technology where sharing, collaboration, social networking, tagging, and voting is the norm. Millennials freely tag legal documents in the company's documents management system. They contribute like mad to blog posts and wikis, given half a chance, and they subscribe to RSS feeds. These activities won't likely replace the old-fashioned office meeting, but partners and managing lawyers must better understand and find creative ways to take advantage of these communication tools in order to get the most from their younger workforce.

Executives and managers in all industries must develop tolerance for and understanding of generational influences before successfully encouraging tolerance in their employees. You need to understand that different generations have different values and motivators and that these motivators must be factored into your management training program.

Many employee conflicts result from an inability to appreciate another generation's point of view. To complicate matters, management style can dramatically affect worker productivity. As a manager, adapting your personal style is critical to supporting effective interactions between generations. Some key generational lessons for managers include knowing what motivates your team, remaining objective, being flexible with your company's standard procedures, and learning ways to leverage the strengths of each group.

Generational Training for Employees

Once you've gotten your management team trained on generational issues, it's time to get down to the business of training your employees. So how do you train four different generations? The answer is one at a time. Each generation has its own learning preferences. Traditionalists appreciate logic and do best when the training is at a reasonable pace, Boomers prefer coaching, Xers love training any way they can get it, and Millennials want to be mentored.

The biggest challenge for most companies is in how to train the flood of young Millennials entering the workforce. Sterling Bank, one of the largest locally managed banks in Texas, hires between twenty and thirty college grads a year, and the company has discovered that younger workers want to be trained quickly, using technology, and without a lot of corporate mumbo-jumbo. Tell them what you expect, show them how to do it, and nothing more. Millennials are highly motivated and hard working, but because they have grown up with technology, video games, and to a lesser degree, reality television, they learn differently. You couldn't pay this group to read a manual during training.

Millennial grads can't be trained the way you trained Xers and Boomers only a few years ago. They have a different take on why training matters. They expect to be improved and challenged. They want learning today that will pay off tomorrow. And somewhat counterintuitively, they want learning today that will benefit their long-term careers. They are sponges for learning and quality matters. Entertaining and engaging training is even better. Do training the right way, and you'll retain Millennials even if other aspects of your organization are less than encouraging—say low pay, nonexistent work-life balance programs, and antiquated and rigid policies, all of which will drive your Millennial workforce crazy. Millennials are keen to learn on the go, so why not enhance your technology-based learning—e-learning, online-learning, multimedia learning including audio and video—to meet this need. Embed professional development into the daily, ongoing job responsibilities rather than relying on discrete, formal training sessions.

Xers, on the other hand, take to training in a different way. Xers don't respond to traditional you-talk–they-listen authoritarian educational methods. One of the biggest traps a trainer can fall into is believing that simply by standing up in front of the room you've got something to say that your Xer workforce wants or needs to hear. On the other hand, Xers respect and respond to authority. The catch is that they must perceive that the authority—senior management, supervisors, and trainers—respect them.

Make sure your training topics are relevant—not to you, but to your Xer workforce. Perform training, as well as all other manager-to-Xer interactions, such as enforcement of policies violations, without being condescending.

Here are a few other tips to training your Xer staff:

Keep the training sessions lively. Try not to dally. Xers have a short attention span, and they like it that way. Explain yourself and your qualifications: Xers want to hear from experts, not lackeys. Clarify your purpose by stating right up front why the training is necessary. Be obvious about what's in it for them. If you have to poke fun at anyone, then make fun of yourself. Xers crave honesty. Share the silly mistakes you made along the way. Turn your presentations into anecdotes—short stories that illustrate the good and the bad. Tell stories that are relevant, amusing, and educational. Get Xers involved. Let Xers themselves set the expectations and develop some of the training outlines.

To help bridge generational expectations, companies like Sterling Bank are hiring generational consultants to train management and workers to find a balance between maintaining a professional corporate culture and meeting the needs of younger workers. Other companies offer diversity training courses in an attempt to create a more inclusive workplace. Let's face it, the success of your company's people strategies depends on your ability to address generational challenges and create a mutually beneficial work environment for all generations. Companies that embrace generational differences retain quality employees, appeal to a wider range of job applicants, create a synergy between generations, increase productivity, and compete more successfully. The result is a more efficient workplace and a more successful and profitable organization

"Do you think it might be a good time to 'revisit' our dress code with Güntar?"

Chapter Eight

Monitoring Compliance

"Now more than ever, prevention is the key. The number
of employment-related lawsuits has tripled in the last decade,
and the average cost to defend a case, win
or lose, has grown to $300,000. "

—Ron Chapman, Jr.,
Ogletree, Deakins, Nash, Smoak & Stewart, PC

How long since you last reviewed your company's compliance
program? Regulatory compliance is an ongoing process, yet many
managers let nagging compliance concerns take a back seat to
strategy and profits. Failure to comply with the stifling number of
government regulations can be costly. In 2007, employees filed over
eighty thousand complaints against employers with the US Equal
Employment Opportunity Commission (EEOC), which resulted
in fines of $230 million.

In part, what follows is a cautionary tale with a simple message: Don't let this happen to you. As an employer, the EEOC isn't your only concern. In August 2008, agents with the Immigration and Customs Enforcement (ICE), a division of the Department of Homeland Security, arrested 595 employees at Howard Industries, Inc., an electric transformer manufacturing facility, for identity theft and fraudulent use of Social Security numbers. Days prior, agents arrested twenty-three illegal alien workers at the headquarters of one of California's major wholesale flower growers, The Sun Valley Group. A week earlier, fifty-seven illegal aliens working at Mills Manufacturing Corporation, a Department of Defense contractor, were arrested by ICE agents. In July, ICE agents stormed into Casa Fiesta and arrested fifty-eight restaurant employees on immigration violations and, in another operation, arrested eighteen men working at Colorado Precast Concrete Inc. in Loveland, Colorado, for being in the United States illegally. These are just a few examples of companies with lax or nonexistent compliance controls in place.

And don't think this can't happen to you.

An upscale resort in the Southwest employed over three hundred workers, many of them kitchen and cleaning staff. Turnover was high and so was the pressure to fill the positions. The human resource department—three stressed and hardworking people—had a difficult time understanding and complying with constantly changing regulations, especially in the area of immigrant work documentation, now administered by the Department of Homeland Security.

The resort's problems began with one or two undocumented workers. In just a few years, undocumented workers had become the way things were done. At one point 70 percent of the resort's workforce consisted of illegal alien workers. The human resource staff had done a good job by keeping vital positions filled, even if they filled those positions with illegal workers.

Eventually an outside audit revealed to the senior management team just how much those undocumented employees could cost the company. The fine for hiring undocumented workers from Mexico, India, Canada, or any other foreign country is $250,000 per individual. If, for example, you have one hundred illegal workers and are fined $250,000 per worker, your total comes to $25 million in fines.

The resort was in a horrible bind. They couldn't fire 70 percent of their workforce at once and still keep the company running. They had to recruit to fill jobs currently held by undocumented workers, and they had to pay more for those jobs so they could attract qualified staff. At the same time, the company spent hundreds of hours re-verifying current workers' paperwork and terminating employees who could not comply.

While managers were hiring and training new staff, they had to run two workforces side by side—one workforce of existing, highly skilled, low-paid workers, and a second workforce of higher-paid, new workers. And of course during the process, the senior executives must have spent sleepless nights worrying about being raided by the Department of Homeland Security.

Over the last few years, the government has cracked down on companies who employ illegal workers. In 2006, there were 4,383 illegal immigrants arrested, three times more than those arrested in 2005. And more recently, Swift, Wal-Mart, UPS Supply Chain Solutions, and others have been in the news for paying huge fines for employing undocumented workers. The lesson here is that the penalties for noncompliance with government regulation isn't worth the anticipated benefits of lax or nonexistent compliance controls.

To help resolve employee conflicts before they become regulatory complaints, it is important to engage a qualified management team to support your organization by reducing risk and liability. The types of risks this book most addresses are those interactions and disagreements focused around people issues—generational conflicts, communication, equality, rights, motivation, and stress.

Often managers and employees are too close to the participants of a dispute, too busy, or too inexperienced to conduct an objective assessment of the situation or complaint. Periodic external audits can be a good first step in building a sound compliance and compliant-resolution program. These external audits can provide an objective examination of current compliance policies and establish directions and priorities to fine-tune or revamp your compliance efforts.

Internal Assessment Tools

Some time ago, I developed an assessment tool to help senior executives assess the quality and overall impact of their organization's human resource and compliance program. The assessment is a thorough, interactive appraisal of general practices, processes, policies, personnel, and strategic directions, along with interviews of key management and staff. An additional benefit of an assessment of this type is a possible reduction in your employment practices liability insurance. EPLI covers businesses against claims by workers when they feel their employment rights have been violated.

Whether you conduct the assessments in-house or hire outside consultants, it's essential to address two key areas: your company's exposure to legal action, and the ways you leverage your current human assets to maximize production.

Minimizing legal exposure and maximizing production are two equally important objectives, but the first is probably the most difficult and should be addressed first. Here are the primary pieces of legislation that impact human resource compliance:

1. Civil Rights Act of 1964 (Title VII) and amendments
   a. Pregnancy Discrimination Act of 1978
   b. Americans with Disabilities Act of 1990 (ADA)
   c. 1991 Amendments to Civil Rights Act
2. Age Discrimination in Employment Act of 1967 (ADEA)
3. Consolidated Omnibus Reconciliation Act of 1985 (COBRA)
4. Older Workers Benefit Protection Act of 1990
5. Drug Free Workplace Act of 1988
6. Family and Medical Leave Act of 1993 (FMLA)
7. Health Insurance Portability and Accountability Act of 1996 (HIPAA)
8. Occupational Health and Safety Act (OSHA)
9. Immigration Reform and Control Act (IRCA)
10. Fair and Accurate Credit Transaction Act of 2005 (FACTA)

After conducting a formal compliance assessment, you will want to follow up by talking to people. Take surveys, do formal interviews, and have casual conversations with employees. Ask lots of questions, and pay attention to the answers. Gather and collate the information into a report or document you can share with senior management.

If you are a C-level executive, start by talking to yourself. When was the last time you read your employee handbook or procedures manual? Are you in compliance with all recent government regulations? Do you have high employee turnover? Do you employ transient labor? Have you ever done an audit of your human resource and compliance functions? Do you have a separate and skilled human resource management team?

A good next step is to talk to your human resource and operations staff and ask about the most pressing people issues within your organization. Not all business are alike, and your recurring people issues will not be the same as other organizations' and will likely be different from those in the same industry. It's natural for staff to feel apprehensive about an audit. Encourage management and frontline staff to expose the truth rather than whitewashing over uncomfortable issues. A thorough assessment should also include reading pertinent materials related to your human resource and compliance processes. Or retain an outside firm to augment your internal efforts to provide assistance through this complicated mass of federal and state regulations.

"The new executive assistant needs to
be proficient with the latest software, e-mail
and Internet, capable of taking shorthand . . .
and able to translate what 'OMG-BFF,
LOL, BRB, GTG-THX' mean."

Chapter Nine

Resourcing Your Human Resources

"Emotional intelligence is the ability to manage feelings
effectively, express oneself appropriately, and work smoothly
with other people toward a common goal."

—Bruce Chodosh,
Managing Partner SpectraComm

There is no secret formula for implementing generational
recruiting, rewarding, managing, motivating, and training ideas
raised in earlier chapters. No short cut. No magic wand that will
help speed things along. Turning any idea into practice takes people,
and the group of people most qualified to implement many of these
generationally sensitive programs is your own human resource team.

Your organization's human resource professionals can help
spear-head projects that turn generational conflicts into a

competitive advantage. For example, when Nan Richards came to work for HCA Inc. as director of recruitment in 2001, she had been a human resource professional in the medical field for more than fifteen years. Before she was hired, her perception of HCA, a consortium of eleven hospitals, was that the organization was a small, fairly unsophisticated community of hospitals. "I was totally wrong," she says. "There were great systems and services in place here. The problem was that nobody knew about us. After all, I didn't know much about them, even though I've been in this industry for years. And if I didn't know, I was sure other professionals didn't either."

Richards had a lot of work to do to educate and convince the professional community that HCA was a great hospital system to work for. One of her first tasks was to build recognition within the professional community. To that end, she and her team created an ad campaign that was edgy, different, and unusual for the conservative health care marketplace. HCA's ads were full of wild colors and shapes and created a big splash in the marketplace.

Richards recruited and hired people who were experienced and well-known in the local markets. She and her team put together recruiting processes that dramatically reduced the time from interview to hire. When Richards was hired, HCA had a 50 percent registered nurse (RN) vacancy rate and 187 RN positions to fill, what Richards calls "a terrifying figure." Within five months, Richards and her team had hired 140 RNs, and the vacancy rate dropped to 6.3 percent, saving the organization more than $1 million per month on contract labor.

Since then, the RN vacancy rate ranged between 5 percent and 8 percent for the whole of Richards's seven-year tenure. She accomplished the task by instituting a host of creative strategies. For example, her team created marketing materials that got attention.

She placed articles in trade journals and got to know personally all the media reps who frequently used hospital employees as resident experts. Hospital events were widely publicized, and names and photos of HCA employees routinely showed up in the trade magazines.

Richards created a process for attending professional schools to attract Millennials and Xers, giving talks about career options. She produced a Career Options brochure, which had information on where to go to school, what degrees were available, what duties went with which jobs, and average salaries. In 2007, her recruiting team handed out more than twenty thousand brochures to residents in the areas served by the hospitals.

Richards's recruiting efforts paid off. Nurses at HCA hospitals have since won fifty-eight nursing awards, and Richards advertises these accomplishments every chance she gets. "It draws attention," she says. "I've heard people say, 'Gee, I keep seeing your winners. There must be something going on over there.'"

There Is No One Right Way

There are not enough Nan Richardses to go around. However, large or small, most organizations need a staff of qualified human resource professionals to manage recruiting, benefits, training, conflict and discipline, and other functions. One of the factors you evaluated during the human resource and compliance assessment was whether the size and configuration of your human resource department was sufficient for your company's size and plans for growth. Ask yourself: is your human resource team actively supporting your strategic objective? If not, why not? Lack of commitment? Lack of vision? Lack of resources?

If the answer is lack of resources, then it's time to make changes.

A rule of thumb for human resource staff is one full-time human resource professional for every one-hundred employees. For large companies, a human resource department might include a department head, HR manager, benefits specialist, information systems analyst, trainer, and generalist. Every company has different needs. The goal is to have the right people in the right positions at the right time, all moving in the same direction. You may need to add people, transition people into or out of the human resource department, or engage a consultant to fill the gaps.

When Sandra Yancey, CEO of eWomenNetwork, founded her new company, she didn't have the need or the money to hire human resources staff. eWomenNetwork is a professional business woman's network that supports, promotes, and showcases member's products and services. For the first couple of years, dedicated human resource staff didn't make any sense. "There were so many things I had to spend money on in the beginning," she says. "So anything that didn't bring in money was an extravagance." Yancey felt that if she hired good managers with people management skills, the lack of human resource pros was a non-issue.

And for a while, she was right.

eWomenNetwork is a close-knit organization with almost a "family" feel. As it grew, the traditional human resource duties became the responsibility of the operations director. When the director moved into another position, those duties fell to the newly hired comptroller. At first, it seemed a good fit. Ultimately, it didn't work. "I was always in her office," says Yancey, "working on some personnel issue, which we'd try to solve together. As a former human resource person myself, I had just enough experience to make me think I could run the company and human resources too. Not so."

After weighing her options, Yancey first contracted a professional employment organization to take over benefits, workers' compensation processing, and payroll. It was a start, but soon the company was growing so fast that outsourcing these few duties wasn't enough. Yancey decided to partner with my firm, a full-service human resource consulting practice. Our consultant put systems and processes in place that were consistent with the culture of eWomenNetwork.

"Our human resource partner is completely on board with who we are," says Yancey. "It was the right decision for us to outsource instead of creating an internal human resource division. They have professionals in every aspect of human resources, which wouldn't be possible to have on staff. And I like that I know they will tell me exactly what they think. They're sensitive to my opinions and desires, but they're not going to be swayed by my CEO title. They always give me an honest answer and their best advice. The outside relationship really comes unbiased. I don't have to spend time coddling them and giving them technology upgrades, and they don't take up space in my office."

Human Resource Reporting

Who reports to whom is always a balancing act. In many companies, the human resource function reports to the chief financial officer. This is not always the optimal reporting structure, because human resource management is often about emotions, motivations, resolving personal conflicts, and other soft skills. Finance is all about objective decision-making centered on how to account for and allocate money. These two disciplines are sometimes at odds with each other. Both functions are vital, and the person who often speaks both languages is the CEO. Why not amend your reporting structure to allow the human resources staff to communicate directly to the company leader? This new reporting structure sends a clear message to line management that the human resource function is a deliberate, valued part of the company's overall strategic plan.

Before Jennifer Kaneshiro was hired by the Chickasaw Nation Division of Commerce, the human resource function was seen as an administrative department. In her capacity as chief human resource officer, Jennifer Kaneshiro oversees fifty-two direct reports and in a short two years has turned her department into a valued strategic business partner.

The Chickasaw Nation employs more than ten thousand people, two thousand of them hired within a recent three-month period of dynamic expansion. Kaneshiro oversaw the massive recruiting, hiring, and training project and brought in consultants to help with the workload. Kaneshiro believes that outsourcing certain functions makes sense because specific projects require experts and additional resources. She also knows that organizations need a core human resource team to support employees and provide value to senior leadership.

Kaneshiro built a team within education, finance, operations, and human resources to modernize the Nation's human resource operations. In the past, Kaneshiro's department was asked to process paper. Now line management is asking, "How do I provide training for a weak manager?" Senior managers ask, "How do we create a strategy to find talented individuals to fill management roles?" And it's not just managers who see the new department as strategic and valuable, but employees as well. Kaneshiro's department has taken the lead in communicating the organization's mission to every employee. And that mission is to "Advance the lives of the Chickasaw people through education, health programs, and good jobs."

The primary function of Kaneshiro's department at the Chickasaw Nation is to make sure the right talent are in the right place. Not an easy task. Many of the Nation's workforce are Millennials with little education and even less experience.

"The biggest challenge with younger workers," says Kaneshiro, "is learning to communicate in ways they respond to. You need to understand their values and work ethic, which are vastly different than their elders." Kaneshiro knows how easy Millennials find it to "go next door" if they don't find what they want working for the Nation. "It's simplistic to deny access to Facebook or MySpace and think you've solved a problem," she says. "With this generation, company-wide policies don't work. The solution is to find unique ways of dealing with this very individualistic generation."

Kaneshiro has placed an emphasis on continual improvement. Department heads conduct employee surveys each year for every department. Employees know their feedback is important, and from experience, they see that unpopular issues aren't shoved into a drawer and forgotten. Instead, the feedback is evaluated and acted upon, one reason the Chickasaw Nation is a great place to work.

Import Your Experts

Years ago, when I was the VP of Human Resources and Risk with Snelling Staffing, one of my nicknames was "the Terminator" because I had the ability to terminate employees and treat them with dignity and respect. The problem was that as soon as people saw me coming, they ran the other way. That nickname was also one of the reasons I left this job and became a human resource consultant. I didn't want to be a terminator anymore.

Ironically, one of my current clients uses me for exactly that function. They don't have a person with the skills to terminate employees, and they don't want to brand anyone in-house as "the

Terminator." Transitioning or terminating staff is a good reason for using an outside consultant.

Managing your organization's human resource needs is a difficult challenge, and hiring a consultant is a viable solution. Human resource consultants can help develop and maintain your systems—compensation, benefits, performance management, and executive search. Consultants can help identify knowledge and experience gaps and fill those gaps by providing training on an as-need basis. Specialized services might include regulatory updates on such topics as the Health Insurance Portability and Accountability Act (HIPAA) and legal alerts, updates on the latest employee learning tools, creating reports that identify new methods for productivity enhancement, recruiting, performance appraisals, benefits consultations and sign-up tools, tips on handling people-oriented challenges, and coaching.

As an experienced human resource consultant, Susan Stockton believes that even well-run human resource departments can benefit from strategic outsourcing. Stockton recommends companies consider co-sourcing with a partner who can be called upon when needed. Examples of co-sourcing services include supplementing in-house staff with specialized skills, providing routine assistance to in-house recruiting, and conducting special projects such as career development programs or training and development.

Co-source partners can act as mentors for key issues that may be outside a manager's experience. "Partnering with an outside consultant is a small cost compared to what one lawsuit could cost in terms of time, energy, resources, and money," Stockton says. She works with inexperienced managers and staff to improve their skills. "There are HR people who don't think it's important to be able to read a financial statement," she says. "They think it's all about the warm and fuzzy. But C-level executives don't want to hear about the warm and fuzzy. They want strategic advice with clear recommendations. They want proposals that have a positive impact on the bottom line. They want you to understand and measure your budgetary responsibility."

Stockton teaches human resource staff about organizational responsibility, accounting, and finance. She teaches staff to keep themselves informed, stop pushing paper, and get out of their offices whenever possible and listen to employees, possibly by starting and facilitating committees and focus groups. "HR workers have a hard job," Stockton says. "Regardless of the organizational reporting structure, they work for all departments. Otherwise, they get no respect from anybody."

To illustrate her point, Stockton often tells one of her favorite stories. "I was the HR director for a rapidly growing company," she says. "We needed somebody in marketing and sales who had global experience and could take us to the next level as we searched for an IPO opportunity. We interviewed and hired a guy who was perfect for the job. He was the epitome of the good, all-around salesman and had the ideal image for an American technology company trying to do business in conservative Europe.

"He came down to my office after we'd completed the hiring process. He sat across from me and said, 'I have to tell you, out of all the companies I've interviewed with, you're the first HR person I can honestly say is not an HR puke.'

"I was taken aback. 'A what?'"

"He said, 'I've worked for a lot of big companies where I had absolutely no respect for their HR because the first word out of their mouths was 'No.' They took no time to get to know me. They didn't want to build trust. Their forms were outdated or sloppily copied so you had to write at an angle. Your group has it together, from how you talked to me to how you treated me, all the way down to where I filled out the forms and signed on the dotted line. I hope this hasn't been a fluke.'

"It was a good start to our relationship, and I was able to build upon it. He was under pressure to put a good team together fast, but he had huge challenges in his recruiting efforts. Everybody he hired would quit in about six months. Just when they get up the learning curve and start to know our products, they'd be gone. When I asked him what he thought the problem was, he didn't have an answer. I asked him if I could sit in on his next interview for senior staff and perhaps participate in the process. He was reluctant at first but finally agreed.

"We traveled to London together and had a slew of candidates lined up for interviews. On the first interview, when it was my turn, I asked behavioral and background questions, like 'Where did you go to school?' or 'What do you like about your job?' He thought my questions were fluff.

"When it was his turn, he asked all the technical questions. I noticed that he spent more than half the interview talking about his philosophy. He never talked about how the prospects did their jobs or their philosophy. He never said, 'Give me an example of how you would approach this client. What is a tool you have used?' None of that.

"After the interview, we recapped, and he asked what I thought. I told him I didn't think the candidate was right because of where he spent his time, and what activities he liked didn't seem to jive with what we were looking for. He disagreed with me. 'I like this candidate's philosophy,' he told me. I asked him, 'How do you know? You never asked him. You talked about your philosophy.'

"As we continued to talk about the candidate, he was impressed with how much information I was able to get out of the interview. In fact he was so impressed he asked if he could use my questions and interview the candidates himself. We spent the next week interviewing people. By the time we found our candidate, he told me, 'I get this now. Now I know what I was missing.' It was eye-opening for him what a qualified human resource manager could do. But it took a long time to get there because of his preconceived ideas."

Training and Development

Consultants can also help with training. Your in-house staff must determine which training programs are needed by assessing appropriate groups or teams of workers. The Dallas Cowboys Cheerleaders, for example, uses third-party assessment tools in their training program. The Cowboys' cheerleader organization relies on a personality assessment tool called Core Multidimensional Awareness Profiles. The Core tool enables the team director and cheerleaders to understand individual motivators, demotivators, strengths, and limitations and use this awareness to perform better as a team.

Teamwork is a vital component in the well-being and growth of any organization, but none so much as in the health care industry. As a physician and a leader, Baylor Health Care System's Dr. Carl Couch is familiar with the challenges of working with independent thinkers. Doctors are notoriously highly self-assured and always right. They are trained to be. However, in today's highly complicated health care system, being right isn't always enough. Soft skills like communication, collaboration, and teamwork are equally helpful.

Successful physician management strategies must carefully bridge the two extremes of autonomy and organizational function. At Baylor, Dr. Couch's innovative human resource programs range from physician recruitment and feedback to rewards and mentoring. The mentoring program partners newly hired physicians and nurses with seasoned health care professionals and has been a powerful tool in training new staff while at the same time helping seasoned physicians mature into wise leaders. The mentoring program has helped doctors and nurses improve communication with patients and staff and given doctors an alternative to physician burnout.

Everyone Needs Advice Sometimes

Have you ever had a nagging question and wished you could pick up the phone and call an expert? I offer clients what I refer to as my "HR Hotline," providing on-call support for human resource staff, C-level executives, and key managers seven days a week.

A client of mine gave me the idea. They were a nationwide organization with multiple locations, and they were having a tough time training managers. The result was high turnover and an increase in litigation. By giving each location one dedicated "Hotline" for human resource issues, staff members were able to talk with a pro and in many cases work through the issue within minutes rather than weeks—all without litigation. Each call was documented, and a log of the calls was sent to the management team on a regular basis. The information was subsequently used to identify regional facility trends, which served as the basis for future training needs.

From that beginning, the hotline has since become highly customizable to fit other clients' needs. The hotline is now used for advice on cost-savings ideas, EEOC complaints, morale issues, exit interviews, program feedback, and more. As I say to my clients, "If an employee is going to complain, let it be to us not to an attorney." If someone has a great cost-cutting idea, you can't afford to let the idea linger without acting on it. An added benefit of the hotline is that listening to your staff shows that you value their input.

Even senior executives can benefit from a word of advice every once in a while.

Don Hanratty, president and founder of the Career Control Group, works with organizations to improve performance for key individuals. "We're a talent advisor to senior executives," says Hanratty. "We work with senior-level staff to get 'off-track' talent back on track. The company provides career, development, selection, and succession support.

Hanratty and his consulting team have worked with a wide range of organizations. For a national retailer, Hanratty provided an executive development program for the company's only female senior executive. For a major private university, he orchestrated a confidential search for a senior officer. For a venture capitalist, he selected a best-fit candidate among three finalists based on a detailed assessment and business simulation interview process. For a family-owned business, he assisted the founders in examining a range of succession options beyond the children taking over the business. For a financial services company, he served as a private resource partner and negotiated an agreement for an unhappy executive to leave the company gracefully while utilizing Career Control's Silent Career Continuation service. And for a major employer, Hanratty and team built an on-site career center for fifty redundant employees that resulted in an $800,000 cost savings to the employer and avoided negative public opinion and employee-relations issues.

No matter how you plan to source your human resource needs—through in-house talent, outsourcing, or co-sourcing with specially trained consultants—your human resources team will play a vital role in turning generational differences into a competitive advantage. Today's human resource professionals have mastered the concept of performance, competitive advantage, and value. At a basic level, the value of understanding and using generational differences to your advantage reflects a changing marketplace. In a world of increasingly scarce resources, activities that fail to add value—like restricting technology for Millennials and excessive rules for Xers—are not worth pursuing. No matter how interesting the activity may seem, if your generationally diverse workforce doesn't find value in them, continuing the activity is a waste of time.

The generational value proposition goes beyond conflict management and bridging gaps and understanding generational personalities. This unique mix of generations in the workforce adds value when the work of these four generations coalesces into a product or service that helps customers reach their goals. How this coalescence takes place doesn't matter. Whether your employee's behaviors are based on honor (Traditionalists) or optimism (Boomers) or balance (Xers) or sociability (Millennials) doesn't matter. What matters is that you create an environment with a shared vision—a vision that reaches the hearts of your entire workforce.

Turning Generational Differences into a Competitive Advantage

The insights and suggestions provided throughout this book form the foundation for assessing your company's people strategies against your firm's wider strategic objectives. Turning generational differences into a competitive advantage is about developing your firm's people resources in ways to maximize those objectives. By examining each generation's influences, you are able to understand how each operates within the corporate world, how each inspires understanding, tolerance, and the ability to work together within your organization. Each generation brings a unique perspective to communication, respect, feedback, and management style. Drawing value from these perspectives is no easy task but is nonetheless achievable by creating flexible and often outside-the-box alternatives to recruiting, rewarding, managing, motivating, and training that allow each generation to contribute to company objectives in ways that make sense to them.

In today's knowledge economy, a company's competitive advantage is often as straightforward as the talents, innovativeness, and leadership abilities of its staff. Leadership, in turn, is about translating vision into reality. On the face of it, gaining a competitive advantage sounds simple. In order to boost profits, increase market share, and create dazzling new products, simply recruit and train young visionaries. Coach and mentor them as they mature. And yet according to IBM's Global Human Capital Study 2008 of more than four hundred human resource executives from forty countries, more than 75 percent of human resource executives say they are concerned with their ability to develop future leaders. Complex organizations can't keep pace, much less transform themselves without great leaders.

Given the retirement of experienced Traditionalists and Boomers, companies are placing their growth strategies at risk if they cannot identify and develop the next generation of leaders. In practical terms, this means spotting young leaders within the ranks of your own Xer and Millennial workforce.

As your organization faces the challenge of a changing workforce demographic, new leadership structures are already required. Let's face it, as an executive, no matter how many hours you work, you cannot control all decisions taking place throughout the organization. You can only hope to implement people strategies and processes that encourage employees to make decisions that improve quality, employee satisfaction, and customer service that are consistent with your own vision and strategic intent. This trickle-down leadership effect doesn't happen by accident. It requires leaders at all levels of the organization and of all ages who understand

and have an affinity for the types of generational dynamics that encourage both corporate and personal achievement.

The best approach to filling the leadership void is to involve your younger, emerging leaders in the decision-making process as early as is practical. Nancy Barry, motivational speaker and author of the book *When Reality Hits*, suggests that Millennials are up to the challenge. In her book, she advises young grads to set high standards for themselves from day one on the job. Ask questions, listen carefully, have a plan, and build a consensus of all the qualities of budding, influential leaders.

If you hired effectively and have the right rewards, motivations, and management processes in place, these younger workers are eager to take on greater leadership roles and follow through on existing initiatives. Yes, your younger Xer and Millennial workers may lack experience or even some specific technical skills, but they can bring you perspectives that help better reach employees and customers. The more these younger workers can be encouraged to get involved, the more you can focus on strategy, creating value, and positioning your company for the future.

About the Author

Sherri Elliott is the president and owner of Optimance Workforce Strategies, LLC, a leading human resource (HR) consulting firm. Her original HR studies and articles and her speaking and consulting work have made Sherri a leading voice in helping companies understand and successfully overcome the challenges of a multigenerational workforce. She is a Senior Professional in Human Resources with an Associate designation in Risk Management with over fifteen years of corporate experience. Cited for her insightful research as well as her ability to translate that knowledge into useful and practical advice for leaders, Sherri has become a sought-after speaker and leader in the HR community. *Ties to Tattoos* focuses on turning generational differences into a competitive advantage.

Optimance Workforce Strategies provides a range of services and resources to help companies find, recruit, hire, and keep their best people. Working with companies to adapt their internal recruiting and staffing processes, Optimance helps clients with both standard HR challenges as well as the increasing pressures of managing workforces in a time where even small age differences can represent a vast cultural gap. For more about Sherri or her company, please visit www.optimance.com or www. tiestotattoos.com.